S!NGAPORE
at Random

Originally published in 2011 by Editions Didier Millet
This edition updated and edited by Alvin Tan Peng Hong

Talisman Publishing Pte Ltd
talisman@apdsing.com
www.talismanpublishing.com

ISBN 978-981-14-7601-3

Original Entries Susan Tsang, Audrey Perera

Printed in Singapore

Disclaimer:
Whilst every effort has been made to ensure that the
information contained in this book is accurate for a book
of entertainment and enjoyment, in the event of errors or
omissions, if relevant, appropriate credit will be made in
future printing of this work.

S!NGAPORE
at Random

magic, myths
& milestones

TALISMAN

I have sailed many waters,
Skirted islands of fire,
Contended with Circe
Who loved the squeal of pigs;
Passed Scylla and Charybdis
To seven years with Calypso,
Heaved in battle against the gods.
Beneath it all
I kept faith with Ithaca, travelled,
Travelled and travelled,
Suffering much, enjoying a little;
Met strange people singing
New myths; made myths myself.

But this lion of the sea
Salt-maned, scaly, wondrous of tail,
Touched with power, insistent
On this brief promontory . . .
Puzzles.

– extract from *Ulysses by the Merlion*
(for Maurice Baker)
by Emeritus Prof. Edwin Thumboo

INTRODUCTION

Rather randomly, during a meeting to discuss the publication of my first book *Singapore: A Very Short History*, my publisher Ian Pringle pulled out a copy of *Singapore at Random* and wondered aloud – was there someone who could update and revise it? Someone at the table pointed her finger at me, Ian gave me a copy of the book and some months later, he rang me. This new edition is the outcome of those rather random gestures.

In updating and revising *Singapore at Random*, I wanted to make Singapore look less sensational, less exotic and less tabloid. Rather, I wanted Singapore to be seen as a place that piqued one's curiosity and interest. In other words, Singapore was a quirky place. To do so entailed sifting through existing entries and creating new ones for more balance in the book's content. But before that, fact checking was necessary to bring some of the entries up to date and so was some wordsmithing to ensure stylistic consistency. It was a pleasure to lose myself in mining the books and the Internet for facts and factoids that make Singapore the place it is – a global city state with strong sense of itself, and of course, local flavours and accents.

Singapore at Random is in some ways very much like one of the street foods that Singaporeans love – rojak. A toss-up of turnip, pineapple, fried tofu dressed in a deliciously sweet and sticky prawn paste with a topping made of crushed peanuts, rojak looks entirely random and haphazard. Yet, it is a carefully considered combination of textures, flavours and scents that makes it works wonderfully as a dish.

Singapore at Random is just like this. It is an invitation to treat, a book to dip into or to flip through (or to be read through in one sitting). It is a sketch map that outlines the lay of the land with just enough detail to guide but not so much as to overwhelm. It is a rabbit hole of discoveries to fall into and lose yourself in. Enjoy.

Alvin Tan
31 January 2021

BAD MOON RISING
. . . .

The Chinese believe that the seventh month of the lunar calendar (usually between August and September each year) is when the gates of Hell open, and spirits of the dead wander the earth freely. During this month, it is regarded as taboo to:

- swim in the sea
- go out late at night
- hold family celebrations
- get married
- buy property
- move to a new house
- renovate your home
- wear anything black
- hang your clothes out at night
- keep umbrellas inside the house
- turn around if someone pats you on the shoulder, or if an unfamiliar voice calls your name at night
- step over ashes or offerings
- sit in the front row of a *getai* (public performances of staged events to entertain wandering spirits, literally song stage) as this row of seats is reserved for visitors from the underworld.

SPOILT FOR CHOICE
. . . .

A traveller who stopped by in colonial Singapore had more than a handful of hotels to choose from if they did not fancy Raffles Hotel or found it too pricey for their liking. These were the Sea View Hotel, the Hotel Van Wijk, the Adelphi, the Bellevue, Pasir Ris Hotel, Hotel de la Paix and the Caledonian Hotel.

PRIME MINISTERS

Singapore has had three Prime Ministers since independence. They are:

- Lee Kuan Yew (1959 – 1990)
- Goh Chok Tong (1990 – 2004)
- Lee Hsien Loong (2004 – incumbent)

WE'VE GOT THE QUARRIES

Singapore literally sits on a geographical formation of granite and old alluvium. In the hillier parts of the island and on Pulau Ubin, granite quarries were a common sight. After reaching its peak in the 1960s, the industry gradually shrank in both scale and activity – by the 1990s, the last operational mine in Pulau Ubin was closed. Over time, these abandoned quarries filled with water and the areas surrounding them were covered with vegetation, such as Hindhede Park, Bukit Batok Nature Park and Bukit Batok Town Park. The last of this trio has even acquired the moniker "Little Guilin". Its craggy granite faces, and cliffs bear more than a passing resemblance to its more famous relation in China.

SINGAPORE'S FIRST WOMAN PRESIDENT

In 2017, Halimah Yacob became Singapore's first woman president and the first Malay president since President Yusof Ishak. Halimah, previously Speaker of Parliament, was returned unopposed under the first reserved presidential election, which was reserved for the Malay community. This was legislated for in 2016 to ensure that there would be multi-racial representation perpetually in the presidency. In this instance, there had been no person from the Malay community who had held the office of the president for any of the last five presidential terms.

MEET THE LOCALS
· · · · · · ·

Singapore is often referred to as a multiracial and multicultural society, but in reality, there are more divisions within the ubiquitous Chinese, Malay, Indian and "Others". Local terms for residents of the island show the range of people and its stereotypes. The following terms are commonly used and sometimes derogatory:

- **Ah Beng** – unsophisticated Chinese ruffian, who usually speaks the Hokkien dialect. He tends to follow fashion trends but is often lacking taste. (Beng is a common Hokkien name).

- **Ah Seng** – perjorative term for anybody (therefore connotes a "nobody").

- **Ah Lian/Ah Huay** – female version of Ah Beng.

- **Ah Kong** – Hokkien for Grandpa. Used to address any old person who is too old to be called "uncle".

- **Ah Mm** (pronounced "mmm") – female version of Ah Kong.

- **Ah Pui** – a generic name for a fat person. Hokkien equivalent of "Fatty".

- **Ya-ya papaya** – an arrogant person. "Ya ya" is a slang term for arrogant, while papaya just happens to rhyme.

- **Keng Chio Kia** – Hokkien for "Banana Child", ie "yellow on the outside, white on the inside". In short, a Chinese who takes on Western affectations.

- **Mat Rocker** – a young Malay male who loves heavy metal music, motorcycles and leather jackets.

- **Electro Minah** or **Minah Rock** – Mat Rocker's girlfriend; female version of Mat Rocker.

- **Sua Koo** – Hokkien for "country bumpkin".

- **Buaya** – a skirt-chaser. Based on the Malay word for "crocodile".

- **Helicopter** – a Chinese-educated person.

- **Mat Salleh** or **Ang Moh** – Malay and Hokkien slang respectively for a "Caucasian".

- **Sarong Party Girl** – a local girl who only dates Caucasian men, often abbreviated to SPG.

MAJULAH SINGAPURA

T he National Anthem was written and composed by the late Zubir Said (1907 - 1987). It was launched together with the National Flag and State Crest on 3 September 1959. The lyrics of the National Anthem and its translation into English are reproduced below.

National Anthem

Majulah Singapura

Mari kita rakyat Singapura
Sama-sama menuju bahagia
Cita-cita kita yang mulia
Berjaya Singapura
Marilah kita bersatu
Dengan semangat yang baru
Semua kita berseru
Majulah Singapura
Majulah Singapura

Onward Singapore

Come, fellow Singaporeans
Let us progress towards happiness together
May our noble aspiration bring
Singapore success
Come, let us unite
In a new spirit
Let our voices soar as one
Onward Singapore
Onward Singapore

STICKS AND STONES

O ver the years, the island-state has been on the receiving end of public insults, some from writers, academics and political leaders. The following are some of the more famous slurs.

"There are 211 million people [in Indonesia]. All the green [area] is Indonesia. And that red dot is Singapore."

– Indonesian President BJ Habibie

"Disneyland with the death penalty."

– Writer William Gibson in an article for *Wired*

"Singapore, a country smaller than a piece of snot."

– Taiwanese Foreign Minister Mark Chen

DIE DIE MUST EAT

I n 1997, Singaporean foodie K.F. Seetoh launched the country's first definitive guide to hawker food – Makansutra. Obviously a pun on the name of the famed ancient Hindu text on love making, the guide listed and evaluated Singapore's beloved hawker stalls. The best stalls were deemed "die die must eat" and awarded a "three chopsticks" rating. Into its tenth edition, Makansutra boasts over six hundred food entries, complete with reviews and ratings. Die die must try!!!

RED LIGHT CALLING

N ot-so-squeaky-clean Singapore has at least six unofficial "red light districts" to its name, scattered around the island. While it is illegal to operate a brothel or to solicit in a public place, in practice, prostitution in Singapore is tolerated and strictly regulated by the authorities.

A CLEAR & BRIGHT DAY
·······

Q ing Ming Jie (also *Cheng Meng*) is a major festival for the Singapore Chinese. *Qing Ming* means "clear and bright" - a reference to the early spring weather. It is a time to remember and pay respects to one's deceased ancestors and family members.

During Qing Ming, families come together to visit the cemeteries and columbaria. Offerings of food and drink are made. Joss sticks are lit and paper offerings in the form of 'hell bank notes', clothing and other necessities are burnt. Of late, items such as credit cards, iPhones and passports have been introduced, facilitating travel and communication in the netherworld.

INDIE BOOKSELLERS
·······

I ndependent booksellers have become a fixture in Singapore in recent years. Beyond books, these stores and museum outlets have also become lifestyle destinations and event venues. Support your local bookseller today!

- Art Science Museum
- Asian Civilisation Museum
- Books Actually (Online)
- Basheer Graphic Books
- Cat Socrates
- Grassroots Book Room

- Huggs-Epigram Coffee Bookshop
- Littered with Books
- RISIS @ Botanic Gardens
- Tango Mango
- Wardah Books
- Woods in the Books

BE PREPARED
·······

T he Boy Scouts played a supporting role in assisting the authorities during the 1915 Singapore Mutiny. Much like their founder Lord Baden-Powell had envisioned, they served as messengers, despatch riders and clerks. Scouting soon became prominent in Singapore, with the first school troops set up in 1922. Today, the Singapore Scouting Association oversees about 10,000 scouts ranging from Cub Scouts to Rover Scouts.

SINGAPORE SLING

L egend has it that the frothy gin-and-juice-based cocktail was created in 1915 by Raffles Hotel bartender Ngiam Tong Boon, who was responding to a British officer's challenge. The officer, who fancied a local merchant's daughter, had demanded a tropical drink befitting the young lady. The name was derived from the anglicisation of the *siling*, or "commander" in Hainanese. The recipe was apparently so valuable that it was locked up in a safe at the Raffles Hotel for many years.

Garnish
A slice of pineapple and a cherry

Ingredients
30ml gin, 15ml Heering cherry liqueur, 120ml pineapple juice, 15ml lime juice, 7.5ml Cointreau, 7.5ml Dom Benedictine and 10ml Grenadine, plus a dash of Angostura bitters

Combine all the ingredients (leaving out the garnish), in a cocktail shaker ⅓ full of ice. Shake and strain the cocktail into a long glass ½–⅔ full of ice. Finally, garnish with pineapple and cherry.

Over the years the Singapore Sling has become world famous. Here are a few references to the cocktail in film and television:

- Actor Johnny Depp's character in the movie *Fear and Loathing in Las Vegas* (1998) mentions drinking Singapore Slings while meeting his attorney.

- Actor Brad Garrett's character from the sitcom *Everybody Loves Raymond* mentions in one episode that he does not know how to make a Singapore Sling as he is "not Asian".

- The Singapore Sling is one of Carrie Bradshaw's (played by Sarah Jessica Parker) choice cocktails in an episode of *Sex And The City.*'

Caution: The Singapore Sling comprises about 30% spirits. Do not drive if you're having one!

Sources: *The Sunday Times*, 9 May 2010; The Raffles Hotel

LIFE IN CAMPAIGN CITY
· · · · · · ·

Lifestyle campaigns to make its residents "better" people are common in Singapore. Here is a selection of campaigns since 1968:

Keep Singapore Clean...1968
Stop at Two/Boy or Girl, Two is Enough..........................1972
National Courtesy Campaign..1979
Speak Mandarin...1979
Have Three or More If You Can Afford it..........................1987
Keep Singapore Clean (again)..1988
Garden City...1990
Save Water 1995
Speak Good English 2000
Romancing Singapore 2003
Singapore's OK...2003
READ Singapore...2004
Huayu [Mandarin], Cool 2006
Singapore Kindness Movement 2009
National Healthy Lifestyle..2010
Speak Good English (yet again) [Get it right!]...................2010

SKY HIGH APARTMENTS, SKY HIGH PRICES
· · · · · · ·

S tanding at 156 metres, Pinnacle at Duxton is Singapore's tallest public housing project. With panoramic views of the city and a city centre location, it is no surprise that the apartments went for stratospheric prices on the open market. In 2020, a 95 square metre apartment purchased at S$340,000 in 2004 went for S$900,000 – a windfall for the owners who were expecting to get 'only' S$850,000.

MONUMENTALLY SPEAKING
· · · · · · ·

S ingapore has a total of 73 national monuments. These span a gamut of structures ranging from religious buildings to civic institutions and structures. Singapore's first batch of eight national monuments were gazetted in 1973 by the Preservation of Monuments Board (PMB). Established by an Act of Parliament in January 1971, the PMB was tasked with the identification and gazetting of buildings as national monuments. It has since been renamed Preservation of Monuments and Sites and reconstituted as a division within the National Heritage Board.

OUR SILENT STALKER
· · · · · · ·

O n Boxing Day in 1990, Inuka was born to proud parents Nanook and Sheba. It was quite an occasion for Inuka was the first polar bear to be born in the tropics. Weighing 350 grams at birth, he was named Inuka (Inuit for Silent Stalker) in a nationwide naming contest that drew 10,000 entries and 390 suggestions. Inuka soon became one of the main draws of the Singapore Zoo and he celebrated his sixteenth birthday in style with an ice cake stuffed with apples and fish. In 2018, it was reported that Inuka had slowed down considerably due to ill health. Surrounded by his keepers, both past and present, Inuka was put down in a humane manner on 25 April 2018. He will always be remembered as "an inquisitive soul and a cheeky fellow" who brought much joy to his keepers and those who visited him.

MOST COMMON TREES IN SINGAPORE

Singapore has a land area of 710 square kilometres, with over 2,000 recorded native plant species. There are about two million trees planted along roadsides, in parks and protected nature reserves. In an effort to introduce the local population to the most common trees in Singapore, the National Parks Board launched the "Know Ten Trees" campaign.

- Trumpet Tree (*Tabebuia rosea*)
- Yellow Flame (*Peltophorum pterocarpum*)
- Sea Apple (*Syzygium grande*)
- Tembusu (*Fagraea fragrans*)
- Angsana (*Pterocarpus indicus*)
- Saga (*Adenanthera pavonina*)
- Senegal Mahogany (*Khaya senegalensis*)
- Sea Almond (*Terminalia catappa*)
- Rain Tree (*Samanea saman*)
- Broad-leafed Mahogany (*Swietenia macrophylla*)

Source: National Parks Board

IN SINGAPORE, THE CAR OWNS YOU

Car prices in Singapore are among the highest (if not the highest) in the world due to a bevy of levies and taxes. These include import duties, registration fees and a purchase tax known as the Certificate of Entitlement (COE). Besides paying for the car, a car owner in Singapore contends with high operating costs. As of February 2020, a litre of 95-octane petrol cost USD 1.56. In neighbouring Malaysia, the price of a litre is USD 0.50.

SMOKING CANTEEN

"From effects from 1st July 2006 this canteen is prohibited from smoking."

– A sign found at a hawker centre in Tuas.

RICKSHAWS IN SINGAPORE

Rickshaws were introduced in Singapore on 16 February 1880. Originally from Japan, they were the taxi-cabs of early Singapore and also a primary source of income for thousands of Chinese immigrants in Singapore who hauled these vehicles and their passengers around town. Invented in Japan in 1869, the name "jinrickshaw" is an anglicisation of *jinrikisha*, the Japanese name for the vehicle which literally means "man-powered carriage".

Initially, Singapore's rickshaws were double-seaters. It was only in 1904 that first-class single-seaters were introduced. These had "English wooden furniture" and "Indian rubber-cushion-tyre wheels". Rickshaw pullers could thus earn more while hauling lighter loads. By 1919, the iron-wheeled double-seater rickshaws were phased out.

In 1947, the traditional rickshaw was finally banned and replaced by the trishaw (essentially a bicycle with a covered sidecar).

BIG WHEEL

Wheelchair-bound Singaporean neuroscientist and medical doctor Dr William Tan entered the record books when he completed seven marathons (roughly 295.4 kilometres) across seven continents in under 27 days. He undertook the mission to raise funds for cancer research in children and took 26 days, 17 hours and 43 minutes to finish the courses, starting in Atlanta, USA, on 22 November and ending in Patriot Hills, Antarctica, on 19 December 2007.

Source: Channel NewsAsia, 14 Jan 2008

LOADED SINGAPOREANS

Singapore has the greatest proportion of millionaire households in the world. Forbes calculated the fortunes of Singapore's 40 richest individuals and families (we are Asian and very family-oriented, after all). Here is the list of the top 10 richest in 2010 and 2019.

Names	Net worth in 2010 (US$bil)	Rank	Names	Net worth in 2019 (US$bil)
Ng Teng Fong's family	7.8	1	Zhang Yong	13.8
Khoo Teck Puat & family	5.9	2	Robert & Philip Ng	12.1
Wee Cho Yaw	3.6	3	Eduardo Saverin	10.6
Kuok Khoon Hong	3.5	4	Goh Cheng Liang	9.5
Richard Chandler	3.4	5	Kwek Leng Beng	8.8
Kwee brothers	3.3	6	Wee Cho Yaw	6.6
Zhong Sheng Jian	1.8	7	Khoo family	6.5
Peter Lim	1.6	8	Kwee brothers	5.7
Kwek Leng Beng	1.4	9	Kuok Khoon Hong	3
Lee Seng Wee	1.3	10	Choo Chong Ngen	2.95

Source: *Forbes Singapore's 40 Wealthiest*

SINGAPORE'S FIRST WOMAN MINISTER

Singapore appointed its first female full minister in 2009. Lim Hwee Hwa, who was elected as a Member of Parliament in 1997, was appointed Minister in the PMO as well as 2nd Minister for Finance and 2nd Minister for Transport. Lim subsequently lost her seat in the 2011 General Election and retired from politics. She was named as "Woman of the Year" by local woman's magazine, Her World, in 2009.

WHAT'S ON TONIGHT?

The Substation Theatre .... 108 (seats)
The Arts House Play Den.. 120
The Arts House Chamber.. 200
The Esplanade Theatre Studio 220
Alliance Française Theatre 236
The Esplanade Recital Studio 245
Chijmes Hall 250
Ngee Ann Kongsi Theatre..358
DBS Arts Centre.. 380
Lee Foundation Theatre.. 380
Jubilee Hall, Raffles Hotel, Singapore........................... 388
University Cultural Centre Theatre, NUS....................... 450
DBS Auditorium 579
Suntec Singapore Theatre 596
Drama Centre Theatre 615
Singapore Chinese Orchestra Concert Hall 884
Kreta Ayer People's Theatre 1,118
Sands Theater @ Marina Bay Sands 1,680
University Cultural Centre Hall 1,714
The Esplanade Concert Hall...1,828
The Esplanade Theatre...1,942
Grand Theater @ Marina Bay Sands 2,155
Star Theatre Performing Arts Centre.............................5,000
Singapore Indoor Stadium..12,000

YOU'VE GOT HAIL

I t used to be said that Singapore has seasonal weather – the hot, the wet and the shopping seasons. Wit (or not) aside, there have been some weather phenomena of note. On 25 June 2013, hailstones fell in Bukit Batok in western Singapore. Hailstones were again observed on 14 October 2013.

HAPPINESS, PROSPERITY & PROGRESS FOR OUR NATION

Singapore's national pledge, introduced on 24 August 1966, was redrafted several times before the one used today was decided on. The first two drafts are reproduced here:

- **First two versions:**

  I pledge/reaffirm my allegiance/loyalty to the Flag of Singapore, and to the country for which it stands: one sovereign nation of many freedom-loving peoples of one heart, one mind and one spirit, dedicated to a just and equal society.

  I proudly and wholeheartedly pledge my loyalty to our flag of Singapore and to the honour and independence of our Republic whose banner it is. We come from different races, religions and cultures, but we are now united in mind and heart as one nation, and one people, dedicated to build by democratic means a more just and equal society.

- **Second version:**

  We, as citizens of Singapore, pledge ourselves to forget differences of race, language and religion and become one united people; to build a democratic society where justice and equality will prevail and where we will seek happiness and progress by helping one another.

- **Final version:**

  We, the citizens of Singapore, pledge ourselves as one united people, regardless of race, language or religion, to build a democratic society, based on justice and equality, so as to achieve happiness, prosperity and progress for our nation.

FIRST SINGAPORE FILM IN CANNES

The first Singaporean film to be screened at the Cannes Film Festival was *12 Storeys* directed by Eric Khoo in 1997. The film depicts the events and happenings in a single twenty-four hour day in a block of HDB flats in Singapore.

THE SHORT AND LONG OF IT ALL

O n any given day in 2018, an average of four million bus rides were taken in Singapore. The shortest point-to-point bus service, 902, runs for just 1.1 km, connecting Woodlands MRT station and Republic Polytechnic. One of the longest bus services, 51, connects Hougang Central with Jurong East, meandering across the island for 37.8 km in 150 minutes. During peak hours, the entire journey can go up to 210 minutes due to heavy traffic. In any case, make sure you have an empty bladder before making the cross-island run.

SINGAPORE STAMPS ITS PRESENCE

I n 1966, the Republic of Singapore issued a commemorative set of three stamps - its first - to mark the first anniversary of its independence. The theme for this issue was "Survival in a Challenging Future in a Multi-Racial Society". The stamps, which measured 43 x 29 millimetres, depicted figures of working men against the backdrop of a newly-industrialised Singapore and its public housing.

WET MARKETS

F resh food markets come in the form of the wet market in Asia. Most wet markets open at 4 am and wind down around noon when the produce has sold out. In Singapore, wet markets are a one-stop destination where you can find everything you need, from dried spices to noodles, fresh poultry to frog meat. They are typically divided into a wet area (where the fresh meat and seafood are found) and a dry area (with sacks of herbs, spices, rice and other dried goods).

The crowds, the haggling and the movement of goods make for a hectic, colourful and odorific experience. At the market in Chinatown Complex, you will find fresh fish, eels, frogs and perhaps a turtle or two. At Tekka Market in Little India, customers seek out the best cuts of beef and mutton, and have their curry pastes concocted and mixed to their exacting tastes.

WATER, WATER, EVERYWHERE
. . . .

In water-scarce Singapore, up to two-thirds of Singapore's land area is utilised for water catchment. This comprises 17 reservoirs and a comprehensive network of storm drains and canals. Here is a list of the reservoirs, from the oldest to the newest:

- MacRitchie Reservoir (1868)
- Lower Peirce Reservoir (1912)
- Upper Seletar Reservoir (1940)
- Jurong Lake Reservoir (1971)
- Kranji Reservoir (1972)
- Pandan Reservoir (1974)
- Upper Peirce Reservoir (1975)
- Pulau Tekong Reservoir (1979)
- Murai Reservoir (1981)

- Poyan Reservoir (1981)
- Sarimbun Reservoir (1981)
- Tengeh Reservoir (1981)
- Bedok Reservoir (1986)
- Lower Seletar Reservoir (1995)
- Marina Reservoir (2008)
- Punggol Reservoir (2011)
- Serangoon Reservoir (2011)

IT'S COOL, MR LEE
. . . .

The late Minister Mentor Lee Kuan Yew (1923 - 2015) hailed the air-conditioner as one of mankind's great inventions.

Source: *TIME 100*, Vol 154, No 7/8

THE POPE DROPS IN ON SINGAPORE
. . . .

Singapore Catholics welcomed Pope John Paul II on 20 November 1986 when he stopped by in Singapore as part of an Asia-Pacific tour. This was the first Papal visit to Singapore. With a crowd of 70,000 in attendance, the Pope celebrated Mass at the National Stadium.

IN THE REALM OF THE CENSORS

Singaporeans are some of the world's most enthusiastic film fanatics, and the multicultural population enjoys films from all over the world. However, the films screened in Singapore have to be passed by the Board of Censors. As a rule of thumb, they look out for obscenity, graphic violence and inappropriate political and religious content.

- **1971:** *A Clockwork Orange* was banned for over 30 years before an attempt to screen it was made in 2006. However the ban was not lifted, and a submission for an M18 rating was rejected.*

- **1974:** *The Texas Chain Saw Massacre* has been banned since the 1970s. In 1986, *The Texas Chain Saw Massacre 2* was similarly banned.

- **1980:** *Saint Jack* is the only Hollywood film to have been shot entirely on location in Singapore. It was banned due to extreme nudity and coarse language. However, the ban was lifted in 2006. It is now rated M-18.

- **1988:** *The Last Temptation of Christ* was never allowed to be screened or released in video format due to its controversial religious content.

- **1999:** The movie *South Park: Bigger, Longer & Uncut* shared the same fate as its banned television series.

- **2004:** *Formula 17*, a Taiwanese film, was banned because it "portrayed homosexuality as normal and a natural progression of society".

- **2001:** *Zoolander* starring Ben Stiller, which caricatured a male model turned assassin attempting to kill the Prime Minister of Malaysia was banned out of deference to Singapore's northerly neighbour.

- **2006:** The movie *Borat: Cultural Learnings of America for Make Benefit Glorious Nation of Kazakhstan* was initially banned for the extreme nudity.

* M18 (Mature 18) – Only audiences 18 years and above may be admitted.

HEAR THE LIONS ROAR?
. . . . . .

A pair of stone lions once stood guard at each end of Merdeka Bridge which spans the Kallang River. This pair, dubbed the Merdeka Lions, was commissioned in 1955 by the Public Works Department. In 1966, they were removed when Nicoll Highway was widened. Eventually, they were relocated to the SAFTI Military Institute where they sit at the base of a SAFTI landmark, the 17-storey observation tower. A pair of replica lions was installed at the Singapore Sports Hub in 2019 as part of an educational and heritage trail.

SINGAPORE STONE
. . . . . .

The Singapore Stone was a large red sandstone boulder stood at the mouth of the Singapore River. Split into two, it was about 3 metres (10 feet) tall and 3 metres (10 feet) long. It was carved with an inscription. This inscription – the earliest ever found in Singapore – is now weathered and therefore illegible. Scholars tried to decipher the meaning behind the inscription but their efforts came to nought.

Munshi Abdullah, who chronicled the early history of the British in Singapore, described how various communities claimed the Stone as their own: "The Indians declared that the writing was Hindu but they were unable to read it. The Chinese claimed that it was in Chinese characters. I went with a party of people, and also Mr Raffles and Mr Thomsen (the Rev. Claudius Henry Thomsen) and we all looked at the rock. I noticed that in shape the lettering was rather like Arabic, but could not read it …"

In 1843, the Singapore Stone was blown up to widen the river mouth. Three fragments with inscriptions were salvaged, and one is now at the National Museum. The other two slabs remain in the museum of the Royal Asiatic Society in Calcutta, where they were sent for analysis.

HEATY AND COOLING FOODS
· · · · · ·

W e've heard of hot desserts and cold soups, but Singaporeans go beyond temperature and look at their food as heaty or cooling. These terms come from traditional Chinese medicine and provide a convenient dietary selection tool - what's hot and what's not?

Heaty foods are "yang", and create heat in the body. Excessive heat results in pimples, sore throats, nose bleeds, mouth ulcers and constipation. Cooling foods are "yin" and sap the body of energy, thus giving rise to weak joints and lethargy. Adjust to suit your taste buds and bodily constitution.

Some examples include:

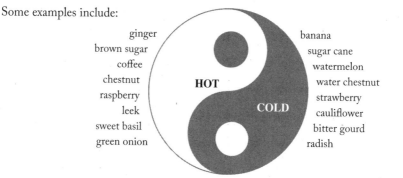

ginger
brown sugar
coffee
chestnut
raspberry
leek
sweet basil
green onion

HOT

COLD

banana
sugar cane
watermelon
water chestnut
strawberry
cauliflower
bitter gourd
radish

STATISTICALLY SPEAKING, THIS IS WHAT INEQUALITY LOOKS LIKE IN SINGAPORE
· · · · · ·

I ncome inequality has become a big issue in recent years. *This is what inequality looks like in Singapore*, an ethnographic study by Singapore academic Teo You Yenn into the lives of low-income Singaporeans, turned out to be a sleeper hit an d national bestseller. In 2019, Singapore's income inequality (as measured by the GINI coefficient) stood at 0.452, down from 0.482 at its peak in 2007. With government transfers and subsidies, the number goes down to 0.398. Singstat, the national statistics office, observes that this shows the "redistributive effects of Government transfers".

THE OTHER WTO
· · · · · · ·

S ingaporean Jack Sim is the founder of the WTO – the World Toilet
Organisation. Sim started locally, by establishing the Restroom Association of
Singapore (RAS) in 1998 to raise the standards of public toilets in Singapore. He
soon realised that there were toilet associations in other countries but there was no
communication among them. The WTO was founded in 2001 with 15 members
across the globe. The WTO is committed to improving toilet and sanitation
conditions worldwide. It was the first global non-profit organisation to be established
in Singapore. In 2005, the World Toilet College (WTC) was formed. The WTO now
has 235 members from 58 countries. Sim's efforts have helped sell 15 million portable
toilets in China and he continues to market potties to the Third World. In 2008, he
was named one of the 30 Heroes of the Environment by *Time Magazine*.

Source: *The Straits Times*, 9 Dec 2009

SINGAPORE CAT
· · · · · · ·

T he common Singapore cat – often derisively referred to as a "drain cat" –
became a tourism icon in 1991. Adopted as an indigenous breed by the
Singapore Tourism Board, it was re-christened "Kucinta" – an amalgamation of
the Malay words *kucing* (cat) and *cinta* (love). Experts speculate that the Kucinta
is a cross between Burmese and Abyssinian cats. It has a richly ticked or agouti
coat which is short, fine-textured and comes in sepia brown
or warm ivory colours, with some barring on the inner front
legs and back knees. It has large ears and striking eyes, which
look like eyeliner has been applied to them. "Cheetah" lines
continue down to its whisker pad and stop before its nose,
which has a clear, dark outline. It is a highly intelligent, lively
and affectionate cat, and makes a loving companion. It is
one of the rarest cats in the world and it is registered as the
smallest recognised breed in the Guinness Book of World
Records. A good specimen can go for as high as US$10,000.

A JOSS STICK'S WORTH OF TALES
· · · · · · ·

Built in 1889, Read Bridge was named after William Henry McLeod Read, a prominent merchant who led the movement for Singapore to be ruled directly from London as a Crown Colony.

Read Bridge is a repository of memories. The most colourful one is of the storytellers who plied their trade there. Chinese migrant workers, especially the Teochews, would gather by the bridge at the end of the work day to listen to these storytellers. Veritable entertainers, they spun tales of folk heroes and legends, and read the latest news to their largely illiterate audience. Each session lasted for the duration of a burning joss stick. As the storyteller began his yarn, he would light a joss stick. And once it was burnt to its end, he would collect his humble fee.

COFFEESHOP CODE WORDS
· · · · · · ·

In Singapore's beloved coffeeshops, a form of verbal shorthand that mixes imagery, pop culture references and the Hokkien dialect is used by the order takers. This shorthand is simple, efficient and effective. Some of these are:

- Tak Giu (踢球) = Milo
- Clementi = Lemon Tea
- Diao He (钓鱼) Diao Yu = Chinese Tea
- Michael Jackson = Chin Chow and Soy Bean Milk
- Ji Ba Ho (一百号) = 100 plus
- Ah Huey (啊花)= Chrysanthemum Tea
- Lao Hor (老虎) = Tiger Beer
- Orh Gao (黑狗) or 'Ang Ji Gao' (红舌狗) = Guinness Foreign Extra Stout
- Wang Qing Shui (忘情水) = Bottled Water/ Mineral Water

SEDITIOUS TOMBSTONE
· · · · · · ·

A 39-year-old Singapore fish-breeder found himself on the wrong side of the law when he buried his brother. In ordering the tombstone of political dissident Tan Chay Wa, Tan Chu Boon was deemed to have breached the Internal Security Act. With an inscription praising his brother as a communist marty, the tombstone was deemed to contain seditious content.

During his trial in 1983, Tan Chu Boon declared that he had no political affiliations. He did not read the proposed inscription given to him by his brother's widow. Still, he was found guilty because he had "under his control, the tombstone of his brother, Tan Chay Wa, on which was engraved in Chinese characters an inscription which tended to advocate acts prejudicial to the security of Singapore". Tan was sentenced to one year's jail, which was reduced to one month upon appeal.

The following is the offending epitaph:

Martyr Tan Chay Wa came from a poor peasant family. In the seventies, he joined the Malayan National Liberation Front, an organisation led by the Communist Party of Malaya. He contributed all the money that he had managed to save to the organisation, thus manifesting amply the noble quality of a revolutionary warrior. He carried on his work in total disregard of his own personal safety. On 2 June 1979, he was arrested. While in prison, he was cruelly beaten up and subjected to coercive threats and inducement but he remained resolute and unflinchingly dauntless. In the cause of the liberation of the motherland, he was hanged in Pudu Prison in Kuala Lumpur on 18 January 1983 and died a heroic death. At the time of his death, he was only 35. A few moments before he died, he wrote a heroic poem which read:

With heart filled with righteous indignation,
I stand at the gallows and forcefully pen this
poem with blood.
I want to air my grievances for a hundred
years,
unable to tell all the wrongs with blood.
When will this gallows be destroyed to
bring about a new heaven?

A PLACE CALLED HOME

Street and building names in Singapore are regulated by an extensive range of rules. These reduce confusion and ensure that names are "unique, reasonably short and easy to pronounce, spell and remember". Some property developers have taken this to ironic extremes to comply with these rules. Here are some examples:

- D'Zire
- Thr3e Thre3 Robin
- Jool Suites
- Tresalveo
- L'viv

- Vogx
- Cradels @ Balestier
- The Levelz
- A Treasure Trove
- Levenue

GIRL, WHY YOU STILL NOT MARRIED?

When children reach a certain age and are still single, Singaporean parents often get a little anxious. They may even try to help things along by sussing out possible matches for their offspring.

In this respect, Singapore, often called a nanny state, might be better described as a parent state. In the 1980s, the government fretted over the large number of its single university-graduate women. It was thought then that this would dilute the national gene pool. To solve this problem, it started a matchmaking service - the Social Development Unit - in 1984. Sardonically renamed "Single, Desperate & Ugly" by its detractors, it tried to pair single graduate women off with single graduate men.

GANTRIES GALORE

There are a total of 93 Electronic Road Pricing (ERP) gantries in Singapore (as of 2018), 36 of which are located in the Central Business District. The ERP is a road usage fee used to manage traffic congestion.

HISTORICAL BUILDINGS IN SINGAPORE
• • • • • •

Architect	Building
George Drumgoole Coleman	Armenian Church of St Gregory the Illuminator

Located on Hill Street, the building was completed in 1835. The Armenian Church was built in the British Neo-Classical style, and was modelled after St Gregory's Church in Echhmiadzin – the mother church in northern Armenia – but adapted to suit Singapore's climate.

Colonel Ronald MacPherson	St Andrew's Cathedral

Completed in 1837, rumours of unhappy spirits and lightning damage resulted in the closure and subsequent demolition of the original church. The new church was consecrated in 1862, and expresses affiliation with the mother Anglican church in England through symbolic objects – the Canterbury Stone, Cross and the Coronation Carpet.

Denis Lesley McSwiney	Cathedral of the Good Shepherd

Consecrated in 1847, the cathedral is oriented eastwards, with the main altar facing the direction of the rising sun. Above the middle entrance is a statue of Jesus carrying a lamb; the inscription below it reads, "I am the Good Shepherd".

Denis Santry	Sultan Mosque

The mosque was first constructed in 1826 with a two-tiered pyramidal roof, typical at the time. In 1928, it was rebuilt and Santry adopted a Saracenic style, incorporating domes, minarets and balustrades. It was gazetted as a national monument on 8 March 1975.

Brother Lothaire Combes	Singapore Art Museum (former St Joseph's Institution)

Completed in 1867, the former St Joseph's Institution was one of Singapore's oldest Catholic boys' schools. It was converted into the Singapore Art Museum in 1996 and many of the building's original features have been effectively preserved.

John Frederick Adolphus McNair	Istana

Built between 1867–1869, the Istana means "palace" in Malay, and was formerly known as Government House. Today, the Istana is the official residence of the President of Singapore. It is open to the public only on certain national holidays such as Chinese New Year and National Day.

Source: *Singapore's 100 Historic Places*

WE'RE SURROUNDED!
· · · · · · ·

A sk any Singaporean to identify the islands around Singapore and they will probably name Sentosa, Pulau Ubin and Pulau Tekong. The first two are well-loved leisure spots and the third houses a Singapore Armed Forces camp that most Singaporean men associate with basic military training. It is a little known fact that as many as sixty four offshore islands surround Singapore. These include Lazarus Island, St. John's Island and Pulau Ubin. Off-limits are Pulau Sudong, Pulau Senang and Pulau Pawai, which serve as the Republic of Singapore Air Force's live firing range.

AS FAR AS THE CROW FLIES (AND MORE)
· · · · · · ·

O n 3 February 2004, Singapore Airlines made aviation history when it launched the world's longest non-stop commercial flight connecting Singapore and Los Angeles. SQ20, which was operated by an Airbus A340-500, covered the distance of 14700 kilometres in sixteen hours. Today, Singapore Airlines once again takes the same accolade for its Singapore-Newark route. This flight, operated by an Airbus A350-900 ULR, covers the distance in eighteen hours with a crew of four pilots and thirteen flight attendants in a two-class – business and premium economy only – configuration.

ROYAL FAVOUR
· · · · · · ·

T he bronze statue of an elephant in front of the Arts House at Old Parliament House was a gift from King Chulalongkorn of Siam who visited Singapore in 1871. The elephant statue was originally placed in front of the Victoria Memorial Hall. In 1919, it was moved to a site opposite the Old Supreme Court.

Source: National Heritage Board

NEW MOON
. . . .

The eighth month of the lunar calendar (usually between September and October each year) is devoted to the worship of the moon. This month is associated with mooncakes, a traditional round pastry filled with lotus paste and melon seeds. Recently, the traditional recipe has been tweaked with the introduction of new textures and flavours. A random selection of flavours include:

- Chocolate yoghurt and bean paste
- Oreo cream cheese
- Ginger-infused "milk snow skin" with century egg and custard paste
- French *cerises griottes* soaked in kirsch paired with white chocolate truffle and mocha paste
- Martell Cordon Bleu Cognac truffle and white lotus paste

THE HARDY TEMBUSU
. . . .

The Tembusu (*Fagraea fragrans*) is a very impressive native hardwood tree according to E.J.H. Corner in *Wayside Trees of Malaya*. It can reach a height of 40 metres (130 feet) and live for over a hundred years. In the past, its durable wood was used for chopping boards and its forked twigs were valued by children, who turned them into slingshots.

The Tembusu flowers twice a year, in May and October, when it is covered with bunches of light yellow flowers. Interesting, the Tembusu flowers gregariously – all the trees flower together. The flowers emit a fragrance which is particularly strong at night. Small round orange berries turn red as they ripen between September and January. These are commonly eaten by bats and birds. The Tembusu is also clad in a distinctive fissured bark.

Some fine specimens can be found in the Singapore Botanic Gardens, where they were standing even before the gardens were founded. One of the trees at the Botanic Gardens is pictured on the back of the Portrait Series $5 note.

The slow-growing Tembusu is now a protected species. It cannot be cut down without permission from the authorities, even if it stands on private land.

BAD PRESENT IDEAS
· · · · · · ·

Singaporeans have a list of taboos when it comes to gifting. Do give it a thought before you send someone a clock for his birthday.

For Chinese

- Clock – The Chinese term for gifting a clock is "song zhong", which is tonally similar to the phrase "to send someone on their last journey"

- Knife – It is considered very bad luck to give someone a knife; it symbolises that the friendship will be "cut off". Collect a token payment (usually ten cents) if you really have to give that set of kitchen knives for Christmas.

For Muslims

- Alcohol – Alcohol consumption is prohibited in Islam. As perfumes usually contain alcohol, these must not be gifted. Liquor or spirits are of course a strict no-no.

- Pigs - Pigs are regarded as unclean in Islam. Items containing pork or pig-derived products must never be gifted.

For Hindus

- Frangipani flowers – Hindus use these flowers only for funeral wreaths. They should not be used in a floral bouquet for a friend.

- Cows – For Hindus, the cow is a sacred animal. Items containing beef or cow-derived products should never be given as presents.

RUN FOR THE HILLS
· · · · · · ·

The outbreak of the COVID-19 virus around the world triggered some remarkable behaviour in Singaporeans. As the Ministry of Health raised the island's alert level to orange on 7 February 2020, Singaporeans decided that it was a good time to stock up on essentials such as instant noodles, rice, hand sanitizer, toilet paper and of, all things, condoms. This wave of panic-buying led to a run on the supermarkets, which were unable to replenish their shelves quickly enough to deal with the sudden surge in demand.

WHERE THERE WERE ORCHARDS
• • • • • • •

Agriculture has played a significant role for much of Singapore's early history. A great deal of the original forest cover was cleared for agriculture.

- **Nutmeg** – one of the first crops planted by the British East India Company in an attempt to break Dutch monopoly of the spice. Nutmeg production in Singapore peaked in the middle of the 19th century, but declined due to an outbreak of disease and falling prices because of oversupply.

- **Gambier** – grown by Chinese farmers even before Raffles founded Singapore. Also known as catechu, this is a common ingredient used by Asians in chewing betel nut. Besides having to clear forest to plant the crop, more forest had to be cut down to boil the gambier leaves to extract tannin for tanning leather and dyeing cotton. The plant also exhausted the land after a few harvests. The planting of gambier stopped only when synthetic compounds were invented.

- **Pepper** – this spice was grown together with gambier, and created a few "pepper and gambier kings" who amassed fortunes.

- **Pineapple** – this fruit replaced pepper and gambier when the international prices of both commodities fell in 1897. By 1901, pineapple was the main crop grown in Singapore.

- **Rubber** – seeds were brought to Singapore in 1877 from the Royal Botanic Gardens of Kew, England. Henry Ridley, botanist and director of the Singapore Botanic Gardens from 1888 to 1911, invented the tapping method that made planting rubber viable, and this technique is still used today. Rubber gained importance as a cash crop, and by 1935, covered about 40 per cent of the island.

Source: National Parks Board

Nutmeg   Gambier   Pepper   Pineapple   Rubber

SINGAPORE'S ROBIN HOOD
· · · · · · ·

Habib Noh bin Mohamad Al-Habshi, aka Syed Noh bin Mohamad Alhabshee, is believed to be a direct descendant of the Prophet Mohammed. He arrived in Singapore as a missionary shortly after the British founded a settlement there.

Most of the tales of Habib Noh centred around his kindness and miraculous powers. He is said to have walked through the rain, from his home in Telok Blangah to heal a sick child in Paya Lebar, without getting wet. He was a Robin Hood of sorts, often walking into shops, taking all the money and distributing the cash to children, with whom he is said to have a strong affinity. Strangely, some shopkeepers did not mind his act.

Habib Noh is also said to have been able to appear in several places simultaneously, faithfully going to Mecca to pray every Friday. The British tried to put him in jail several times, but gave up as he would disappear from his cell.

After a lifetime of caring for the poor and destitute, he passed away in 1866. It is said that his coffin could not be lifted until someone remembered his wish to be laid to rest at the peak of Mount Palmer, where he used to meditate. The Parsi who was said to own Mount Palmer and was reluctant to have a tomb on it, demanded a huge fee to allow Habib Noh's *maqam* (tomb) there. The money was raised speedily, but the Parsi died three days later. The piece of land was bought over and Habib Noh was buried there as he had wished.

In 1890, a mausoleum with 49 steps was built by Syed Mohammed bin Ahmad Alsagoff to commemorate him.

MOBILE IN 1988
· · · · · · ·

The earliest mobile telephone service in Singapore was launched in 1988. The early handphones weighed around 600–700 grams and were priced between $2,900 and $3,400.

RED SCARVES

Recognisable from the blood-red 'scarf' (a square of red cloth folded to sit like a large rectangular roof) that provided a measure of protection from the sun and served as a carry-all, the Samsui women were known for their resilience, hardiness, thrift and austerity. Together with their black samfoo and footwear made from cut-up rubber tyres, the Samsui women were a familiar sight in Singapore.

Originating from Sanshui county in Guangdong province in China, the Samsui women came to Singapore in large numbers during the 1930s. During this time, the British placed strict quota limits on the number of male Chinese immigrants. Women were however exempt and hence, these Samsui women took their place instead.

The Samsui women were employed in the construction and building industry in Singapore on work sites to carry building materials and remove debris. They tended to work well into old age, some even into their seventies, sending most of their earnings back to China and keeping little for themselves.

Today, these hardy women are a rarity – their numbers have dwindled as most have either retired in China or have passed away. They have however been remembered in many ways –one of the merchandise items carried at the Singapore branches of Starbucks is a teddy bear dressed in trademark samfoo and red scarf.

Source: National Library Board Infopedia Talk

3 PLACES OUTSIDE SINGAPORE YOU CAN GET TO IN AN HOUR

Place	Duration (minutes)	Mode of Transport
Bintan, Indonesia	45–50	Ferry (from Tanah Merah Terminal)
Batam, Indonesia	50	Ferry (from Harbourfront Terminal)
Kuala Lumpur, Malaysia	55	Aeroplane (from Changi Airport)

HENDERSON MAKES WAVES
· · · · · · ·

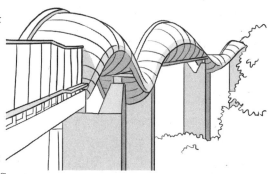

O pened in 2008, Henderson Waves Bridge is the highest pedestrian bridge in Singapore. Spanning 274 metres and standing at 36 metres above Henderson Road, it connects Mount Faber Park and Telok Blangah Hill Park. Its wooden deck is made of the all-weather balau wood, commonly found in Southeast Asia. Seven undulating curved steel ribs alternately rise over and under its deck. The curved ribs create alcoves that serve as rest areas for tired walkers or as a cosy nook for courting couples who want to admire the stars at night.

A signature landmark of the Southern Ridges trail, the bridge is a striking visual statement as it snakes it way above Henderson Way.

SO WHAT DID YOU BUILD TODAY?
· · · · · · ·

I f you have ever been to Singapore's National Gallery (housed in the former Supreme Court) or marvelled at the graceful lines of the Kallang Airport terminal building, then you have been to a building designed by Frank Dorrington Ward (1885 – 1972). Ward arrived in Singapore in 1920 and was appointed chief assistant architect in the Public Works Department, becoming chief architect in 1928. Ward turned out to be extraordinarily prolific and creative as an architect. In a little over a decade, Ward designed the Hill Street Police Station, Clifford Pier, Custom House, Drill Hall and the police station at Robinson Road. Many of his creations still stand today and have been designated as national monuments. Ward left Singapore in 1939 and was conferred the Order of the British Empire (OBE) in 1941 in recognition for his architectural work in the Straits Settlements.

BIG TROUBLE IN LITTLE INDIA
· · · · · · ·

Singaporeans watched in disbelief as footage of a riot in Little India was splashed across their television screens on 8 December 2013. Not since the 1950s and 1960s had Singapore seen such a display of public violence and blatant disregard for law and order. Some 240 police officers were deployed to quell the riots, which were eventually put down. A commission of inquiry was subsequently tasked to look into the event and identify its causes as well as evaluate the response of law enforcement agencies.

ONE BIG FAMILY
· · · · · · ·

There are more than 190 members in the Singapore Federation of Chinese Clan Associations. Here are the founding members who represent the major dialect groups of Singapore's Chinese community:

- Singapore Hokkien Huay Kuan (Hokkiens)
- Teochew Poit Ip Huay Kuan (Teochews)
- Singapore Kwangtung Hui Kwan (Cantonese)
- Nanyang Khek Community Guild (Hakkas)
- Singapore Hainan Hwee Kuan (Hainanese)
- Singapore Sam Kiang Huay Kuan (immigrants from the Zhejiang, Jiangsu and Jiangxi provinces of China, otherwise known collectively as Shanghainese)
- Singapore Foochow Association (Hockchews)

Established on 27 January 1986, the federation aims to strengthen cooperation among the clan associations, organise and support educational, cultural and community activities, and promote Chinese language, culture and traditions.

MEET OTHER SINGAPORE "RESIDENTS"

· · · · · ·

Name	Description
Pontianak	The *pontianak* is a vampiric spirit that is said to be the spirit of a woman who died during childbirth. Most of the time she looks beautiful, but if you look closely, she actually has sharp teeth. She tends to come out after the sun sets to search for victims – normally men or pregnant women. Some say that she rips babies out of their mothers' wombs for food.
Toyol (or Tuyul)	A *toyol* is the spirit of a dead foetus that is kept to steal from others. This spirit is kept in the form of a foetus in a jar. To get the *toyol* to do one's bidding, the owner has to feed it with his own blood daily.
Polong	An unseen ghost enslaved by *bomohs* (black magic practitioners) to harm others.
Pelesit	A spirit which can turn itself into a grasshopper that *bomohs* use to possess someone to extort money.
Hantu Air	Usually someone who has drowned, this is a water ghost associated with rivers, ponds and even swimming pools.
Kum Kum	A banished spirit who preys on virgins to restore her own youth and beauty.
Hantu Raya	A ghost which can confer great powers on its master and act as a *bomoh*'s double.
Hantu Tetek	A female ghost who uses her huge breasts to suffocate people.
Orang Bunian	A benign ghost who usually inhabit the forests, and is known to help humans in trouble.
Hantu Bungkus	A ghost that appears wrapped in a white shroud. It is also known as *pocong*.
Hantu Bukit	A *hantu bukit* is a ghost believed to roam and haunt hills.

Hantu Jepun	A headless Japanese ghost dressed in World War II-era military uniform, often seen marching, while carrying a samurai sword or a rifle.
Hantu Pari-Pari	A *hantu pari-pari* is a fairy.
Hantu Kubur	It is a ghost that loiters in and around cemeteries.
Orang Minyak	Known as "oily man", he is usually seen covered in black oil and is said to rape virgins.
Hantu Penang-galan (Hantu Tengelong)	A female ghost that can separate her head from her body, and fly with her guts hanging out. She is said to love sucking blood from women in labour.

I WANT MY BAG AND I WANT IT NOW

A t Changi Airport, the first luggage bag has to be on the baggage-claim belt by the 12th minute from when the plane docks, and the last bag by the 29th minute.

SCRAPS, ANYONE?

D uring the Japanese Occupation (1942 - 1945), leftovers at Chinese restaurants would be boiled down and sold. Known as 'dish ends', they were sold to customers who brought their own mugs or bowls to take these leftovers away. This reclaimed stock was then used to add flavour to meagre meals. And whenever the remnants turned up a sliver of chicken, a few strands of shark's fin or a small clump of bird's nest, it was a small moment for rejoicing in food-scarce wartime Singapore.

Source: *Wartime Kitchen: Food and Eating in Singapore 1942–1950*

THIS IS ENGLISH?
. . . .

arrow

Origin: English

Meaning: to be assigned an undesirable task by a superior, usually as a subtle passive-aggressive form of punishment

Example: Wah lau! Just because I never come for meeting ... my boss **arrow** me to do this job.

Translation: Oh man! Just because I didn't go to the meeting, my boss singled me out for this job.

kan-cheong

Origin: Hokkien

Meaning: to be hurried, flustered, uptight

Example 1: The MRT door heaven open yet, you so *kan-cheong* for what?

Example 2: Now ownee Apler, Novembler then exam, why so *kan-cheong*?

Translation 1: The MRT doors haven't even opened yet, why are you in such a hurry to get out?

Translation 2: It's only April now, the exam's in November, why are you so stressed out?

kiasu

Origin: Hokkien

Meaning: fear of losing out

Example: (At a buffet line) Why you so *kiasu*? Take so many. After can take again what.

Translation: Why are you so greedy? You've taken so much food. You can always take more later.

oso can

Origin: English (direct translation from Mandarin)

Meaning: Standard answer given when one does not really want to make a decision.

Example 1: Can you send me home?

Oso can.

Example 2: How about go to Bishan?

Oso can.

Translation 1: Can you take me home?

OK.

Translation 2: Why don't we go to Bishan?

OK.

Why you so like dat?

Origin: English (direct translation from Mandarin)

Meaning: Why did you behave in this way?

Example: Aiya, **why you so like dat**? Tell you so many times don't throw rubbish everywhere you also don't listen. So incolligible one.

Translation: Urgh, why did you do that? I've told you so many times not to throw rubbish everywhere, you never listen. You're so incorrigible.

jia-lat

Origin: Hokkien

Meaning: Very serious; prefixed with *see-peh* to accentuate its severity.

Example: I hit someone at the traffic light, ***see-peh jia-lat*** ah …

Translation: I knocked someone down at the traffic light. I'm totally screwed.

Source: Jokedose.com

ABSOLUTELY FABER-LOUS

C aptain Charles Edward Faber of the Madras Engineers arrived in Singapore in September 1844 and was appointed Superintending Engineer (1844 - 1850). He built a narrow and winding road to the summit of Telok Blangah Hill for a new signal station. For all his effort, he was derided in *The Free Press* which declared it a "… stupidly narrow road to the top … two persons meeting can barely pass each other …" Stupid or not, Faber still managed to have the hill named after him.

The list of Faber's follies continues. Ellenborough Market, built in May 1845, was criticised for shoddy construction. Barely a year later, it started to sink due to poor foundation work as cracks soon appeared on the walls. And to fix an overly low bridge spanning the Singapore River, Faber recommended dredging the river while leaving the bridge in place.

MORE THAN ONE SINGAPORE

T here is more than one Singapore in the world, it seems. There used to be a town in Michigan in the United States that was called Singapore, cited as "perhaps Michigan's most famous ghost town". Singapore, Michigan, reportedly home to 150 people in the mid-1800s, was reportedly buried in a sand storm. There is also a small town in South Africa called Singapore, located in the Limpopo province. And in India there are two settlements named Singapur.

Source: *The Straits Times*, 8 Aug 2010

LET'S GO FOR A PICNIC

P ractically a part of every Singaporean's daily life today, Singapore's first food court opened in 1985 at Scotts Shopping Centre. Aptly named "Picnic", it served local hawker food at reasonable prices and air-conditioned comfort. This triggered a trend and, very soon, food courts were all over the island. When Scotts Shopping Centre was redeveloped in 2006, the "Picnic" closed its doors for good.

BRING YOUR OWN?
． ． ． ． ． ．

Singaporeans take home some 820 million plastic bags each year. This works out to 146 plastic bag per person in Singapore every year. Only 4% of plastic waste is recycled and the rest is either burnt off, buried in a landfill or exported for 'disposal' overseas. In 2017, a non-profit NGO, Zero Waste Sg started the Bring Your Own (BYO) Singapore movement that involved 430 retail outlets and reduced the use of plastic disposables by 2,500,000 pieces. By 2019, 881 retail outlets were onboard.

IT'S ALL IN THE MIND (NOT)
． ． ． ． ． ．

The 2016 Singapore Mental Health Survey reported that 6.3% of Singaporeans suffered from major depressive disorder, 3.6% had obsessive compulsive disorder and 4.1% were dependent on alcohol.

STAYING ROOTED
． ． ． ． ． ．

Older Singaporeans who lived through and survived the Japanese Occupation (1942 - 1945) have passed on a fair share "tapioca tales" to their descendants. Food was so scarce that people grew tapioca as a rice substitute and a food source. Tapioca had the virtue of being easy to plant – just shove a tapioca stick into the ground (it doesn't even have to be good ground) and wait for a decent interval before pulling it up. Hopefully, there would be a few little tubers on the end.

Tapioca stories were usually told to remind their young listeners how fortunate they are, or to persuade finicky young ones to finish the food on their plates.

Source: *Wartime Kitchen – Food and Eating in Singapore 1942–1950*

ON THE FIRST DAY OF CHRISTMAS...
• • • • • • •

On 25 December 1643, Captain William Mynors of the East India Company sailed past a small mote of land in the Indian Ocean and named it Christmas Island, perhaps as an afterthought. Some two hundred and fifty years later, the island was home to about a thousand people, most of whom were Chinese labourers mining its rich phosphate veins. And while Singapore administered it as part of the Straits Settlements from 1900, Christmas Island's sovereignty was vested in Britain.

With its geopolitical interests at heart – the island's rich phosphate mines and strategic location were irresistible – Australia acted to acquire Christmas Island from Britain in 1955. Singapore, as the island's administrator, could do little except voice its concerns over the loss of phosphate revenue and the status of its inhabitants.

On 1 October 1958, Christmas Island was transferred to Australia and a compensation of M$20 million was paid to Singapore. Lim Yew Hock, then Singapore Chief Minister, went down in history (somewhat unfairly) as the man who "sold" Christmas Island when it really wasn't his to "sell" to begin with.

Today, Christmas Island is known for its spectacular mass migration of red crabs (*gecarcoidea natalis*) that takes place with the first rainfall of the wet season. From 2001 to 2018, it was used by the Australian government as an "immigration reception and processing centre" to hold asylum seekers attempting to reach Australia by boat.

A little trace of Singapore remains on Christmas Island though. In April 1968, it was reported that a mining company had awarded the HDB a contract to build apartment blocks on the island for its employees. Five of the original seven blocks, which command a sea view, still stand today.

HEY, YOU FILE INCOME TAX ALREADY OR NOT?
• • • • • • •

In 1947, the Income Tax Ordinance was passed by the colonial legislature, paving the way for the collection of income tax. In the first Year of Assessment (1948 – 1949), 40,000 individual tax returns and 1,000 corporate tax returns were received. The taxman took in S$33.2 million that year – the first time any income tax was collected in the colony's history.

PRINCIPAL CAUSES OF DEATH

	2009	2018
Total Number of Deaths	17,101	21,282
Percentage of Total Deaths		
Cancer	29.3	28.1
Ischaemic Heart Disease	19.2	18.1
Pneumonia	15.3	20.6
Cerebrovascular Disease (including Stroke)	8.0	6.0
External causes e.g. accidents	5.7	4.3
Other Heart Diseases	4.4	2.1
Diabetes Mellitus	1.7	1.3
Chronic Obstructive Lung Disease	2.4	1.3
Nephritis, Nephrotic Syndrome & Nephrosis	2.3	3.0
Urinary Tract Infection	2.5	1.3

Source: Ministry of Health

FIRST SINGAPOREAN AIDS VICTIM COMES OUT

Paddy Chew (29 March 1960–21 August 1999) was the first Singaporean to publicly identify as HIV-positive. Chew, who also declared himself bisexual, did so on 12 December 1998 at the first National AIDS Conference in Singapore.

The former flight attendant also wrote and acted in an autobiographical play, *Completely With/Out Character*. The proceeds went to Action for AIDS, a non-governmental organisation focused on AIDS prevention and education.

To those who criticised him as a publicity seeker, he said: "I do not mind being famous for winning the Miss Universe crown, or as a singer, or a beautiful face, you know? Who wants to be famous for having AIDS? For goodness' sake!"

FUSION YUSHENG
· · · · · ·

Tossing and eating *yusheng*, a raw fish salad, during Chinese New Year, is a uniquely Singaporean event. The brainchild of four chefs at the Dragon Phoenix Restaurant, *yusheng* was devised in 1964 in a bid to attract more customers. A typical *yusheng* consists of thinly sliced raw fish, julienned carrot, cucumber, radish, sesame seeds and crackers, all tossed in a plum sauce and fragrant oil, and garnished with crackers. Some very innovative varieties of *yusheng* have been created, reflecting both global influences and local tastes.

- Peranakan *yusheng* – with jellyfish and a *belacan* (prawn paste) sauce
- Tandoori salmon *yusheng* – with tandoori salmon and chutney
- Japanese sashimi *yusheng* – with a sashimi selection, marinated seaweed and *ponzu* (citrus-based sauce)
- Wagyu beef *yusheng* – with wagyu beef and a soya sauce mixed with sesame oil
- Thai *yusheng* – with green papaya, mango and pomelo, accompanied by a spicy sauce of tamarind, *gula malaka*, lime juice, fish sauce and chilli
- Tropical fruit *yusheng* with lobster and baby abalone – with lobster, baby abalone, salmon, rambutan, passion fruit, kiwi fruit, mango and jackfruit
- Healthy *yusheng* – kale, beetroot, green apple, flax seeds and smoked salmon
- Sichuan *yusheng* – octopus, Norwegian caviar, jellyfish, fresh prawns, abalone and salmon

THINGS JUST GOT A LITTLE COLOURFUL
· · · · · ·

Watching soccer on television became a lot more exciting and vivid for Singaporeans on 7 July 1974. The final of the FIFA World Cup which pitted West Germany against Holland was broadcast in colour, making the match in which West Germany beat Holland 2-1 more memorable than ever.

AND THEN THERE WAS LIGHT
· · · · · · ·

The refurbished main building of the Raffles Hotel, which was opened on 18 November 1899, boasted the very first electric lights and fans in the country.

Source: www.raffles.com

RAFFLES' STATUE FAST FACTS
· · · · · ·

Height:	2.43 metres (8 feet)
Cast by:	Thomas Woolner
Cost:	$20,446.10 (Straits dollars)
Mounting:	Granite
Original site:	The Esplanade, with Raffles facing the sea
Date unveiled:	27 June 1887
Unveiled by:	Sir Frederick Weld, Governor of the Straits Settlements
Inscription (1919) by:	Lim Koon Tye (who won $25 in the inscription competition)
Inscription reads:	This tablet to the memory of Sir Stamford Raffles to whose foresight and genius Singapore owes its existence and prosperity unveiled on February 6th, 1919 to commemorate the 100th anniversary of the foundation of the Settlement.
During Japanese Occupation:	Kept in Raffles Museum (then renamed Syonan Museum)
Post-war:	The monument was re-installed at Empress Place in 1946.

PRESIDENTS
· · · · · ·

Singapore has had seven Presidents since independence: They are:

- Yusof bin Ishak (1965 – 1970)
- Benjamin Henry Sheares (1970 – 1981)
- C.V. Devan Nair (1981 – 1985)
- Wee Kim Wee (1985 – 1993)
- Ong Teng Cheong (1993 – 1999)
- S.R. Nathan (1999 – 2011)
- Tony Tan Keng Yam (2011 – 2017)
- Halimah Yacob (2017 – incumbent)

BEFORE THE FIRST GIRL...
· · · · · ·

The first flight attendant – on Malayan Airways Ltd, which was the forerunner of Singapore Airlines – was a man. He was an air traffic controller who was roped in to serve tea and sandwiches to passengers, while the first six female flight attendants were being trained.

Source: *Chronicle of Singapore 1959–2009*

A THIRSTY NATION
· · · · · ·

Despite being in the rain-drenched tropics and having an extensive rainwater catchment network, Singapore does not have enough water for its needs. Hence, it relies on four 'taps' for its water supply - local catchment, reclaimed water, desalinated water and imported water from Malaysia - a diversified sourcing strategy to ensure there is no over-reliance on one source. Water, a strategic resource, is clean and potable - it can be drunk straight from the tap.

EXTINCTION IS FOREVER
· · · · · · ·

Singapore's rapid urbanisation has led to the inevitable clash between man and nature. Some species that are "presumed nationally extinct" include:

- *Brechites penis* (Waterspout or Watering-Pot Shell)
- *Mesida gemmea* (Jewelled Mesida)
- *Hymenopus coronatus* (Walking Flower Mantis)
- *Coremiocnemis valida* (Singapore Brown Tarantula)

| Waterspout or Watering-Pot Shell) | Jewelled Mesida | Walking Flower Mantis | Singapore Brown Tarantula |

Source: *The Singapore Red Data Book*

WHAT'S YOUR NAME?
· · · · · · ·

The most common Chinese surnames in Singapore are **Tan, Lim** and **Lee.**

23 TIGHT TURNS AND A WEEKEND OF ROAD CLOSURES
· · · · · · ·

The annual Singapore F1 Grand Prix night race roared into Singapore in 2008. This event, a world first, put the island city-state onto the global events scene. With a flood-lit circuit boasting a world-beating 23 turns and the impressive city skyline as its backdrop, it is a spectacle designed to both impress and entertain.

WITH A SONG IN OUR HEART...

O ne of the most enduring and memorable government campaigns run in Singapore is the National Courtesy Campaign. Launched on 1 June 1979 by Prime Minister Lee Kuan Yew, it aimed to "create a pleasant social environment, with Singaporeans considerate to each other and thoughtful to each other's needs". Singaporeans were exhorted to "make courtesy our way of life", as the campaign slogan went. In 1982, the smiling face icon was replaced by the beloved and affable-looking Singa, the Courtesy Lion.

Make Courtesy Our Way of Life
"Courtesy is for free,
Courtesy is for you and me.
It makes for gracious living and harmony.
Giving a friendly smile,
Helping out where we can.
Trying hard to be polite all the time.
Courtesy is for free,
Courtesy is for you and me.
It makes for gracious living and harmony.
Living could be a treat,
If people are awfully sweet.
Courtesy could be our way of life.

It is rude to be abusive,
Just to prove we're right.
Instead we could be nice about it if we tried.

Courtesy is for free,
Courtesy is for you and me.
It makes for gracious living and harmony.
Living could be a treat,
If people are awfully sweet.
Courtesy could be our way of life.
Make courtesy a way of life "

SINGAPORE'S CHIEF JUSTICES

S ingapore has had four Chief Justices since Sir Alan E.R. Rose, the last British Chief Justice, stepped down in 1962.

Chief Justice	Start of Term	End of Term
Wee Chong Jin	5 Jan 1963	27 Sep 1990
Yong Pung How	28 Sep 1990	10 Apr 2006
Chan Sek Keong	11 Apr 2006	5 Nov 2012
Sundaresh Menon	6 Nov 2012	(Incumbent)

BOMBINGS THAT HAVE CAUSED CASUALTIES IN SINGAPORE

1. Aerial bombing of Singapore Town by the Japanese, 8 December 1941: 61 killed, more than 700 injured

2. "Mad Bomber" bombings, 26 September 1963: 2 bombs were detonated in three days at Katong Park.

3. Telephone booth bombing, 16 April 1964: 5 injured when a booth exploded in Kampong Melayu off Jalan Eunos

4. MacDonald House bombing, 10 March 1965: 2 killed, at least 33 injured when a bomb planted by Indonesian saboteurs exploded

5. Car bomb, 30 March 1992: 1 pregnant woman killed, her husband being the believed target for the bomb due to illegal money-lending

THE POST OFFICE SAVINGS BANK

The blue and yellow livery of the Post Office Savings Bank (POSBank today) is a familiar sight to Singaporeans. Founded in 1877 by the colonial government to cater to lower income groups, the POSB grew steadily and had a hefty 14.3 million Straits dollars on its books. In 1972, the POSB became a statutory board and a new brand identity was introduced. Its signature key logo, which was designed around the letters POSB, was introduced the same year. POSB achieved another first in 1981 when it introduced its first ATM, dubbed the "Cash-on-Line" machine. Today, POSBank is part of the Development Bank of Singapore (DBS) which acquired it in 1998 for $1.6 billion. To Singaporeans, however, little has changed – the bank retains the same look that they have come to identify with banking services.

CHANGING VIEWS

Today, the road fronting Raffles Hotel – Beach Road – was so named because it was literally the coastline of Singapore.

MISUSE OF DRUGS ACT

Under the Misuse of Drugs Act, unless authorised by the government, the possession, consumption, import, export, or trafficking of controlled drugs are illegal. The list of controlled drugs includes (but is not limited to):

- 100 g of opium
- 3 g of morphine
- 2 g of diamorphine
- 15 g of cannabis
- 30 g of cannabis mixture
- 10 g of cannabis resin
- 3 g of cocaine
- 25 g of methamphetamine
- 113 g of ketamine; or
- 10 g of any or any combination of the following:
  - N, α-dimethyl-3,4-(methylenedioxy)phenethylamine
  - α-methyl-3,4-(methylenedioxy)phenethylamine or
  - N-ethyl-α-methyl-3,4-(methylenedioxy)phenethylamine

Any person who is proved to have had in his possession more than the above quantities, whether or not contained in any other substance, shall be presumed to be in possession of that drug for the purpose of trafficking unless it is proven otherwise.

The death sentence is mandatory for any person caught in unauthorised trafficking of the following:

- more than 1,200 g of opium and containing more than 30 g of morphine
- controlled drugs (except opium) containing more than 30 g of morphine

- controlled drugs containing more than 15 g of diamorphine
- controlled drugs containing more than 30 g of cocaine
- more than 500 g of cannabis
- more than 1,000 g of cannabis mixture
- more than 200 g of cannabis resin
- controlled drugs containing more than 250 g of methamphetamine being.

Extracted from the Misuse of Drugs Act 1973 (Chapter 185), Attorney General's Chambers

THE SULTAN'S MOSQUE

The largest mosque in Singapore, Sultan Mosque, had illustrious beginnings. It was named after Sultan Hussein Shah of Singapore. While residing at the Istana Kampong Glam, he requested that a mosque be built nearby. To this end, Raffles pledged $3,000 of the East India Company's money to help build it. The original building, put up in 1826, was demolished to make way for the current building, which was completed in 1932. It was designated a national monument in 1975.

Source: National Heritage Board

LET ME THINK ABOUT IT

In a bid to ensure that voters had time to think over their choices (and the implications of their choices), the Singapore government introduced the Cooling Off Day in 2010. On Cooling Off Day, political campaigning, canvassing for votes and election meetings are disallowed. The first Cooling Off Day was on 6 May 2011.

PESTA SUKAN
· · · · · · ·

From 1964 to the 1980s, Singapore had its own mini-Olympics in the form of the Pesta Sukan (Sports Festival in Malay). The first edition was held from 4 – 12 December 1964, when Singapore was part of the Federation of Malaysia. Pesta Sukan was mooted to promote racial harmony and encourage a greater interest in sports. The programme included athletics, basketball, boxing, chess, cricket, cycling, football, go-karting, golf, hockey, judo, motor-racing, polo, rugby, sepak-raga (or "sepak takraw"), softball, swimming, table tennis, volleyball, weightlifting, wrestling and yachting. In 2019, the Pesta Sukan was brought back as part of Singapore's Bicentennial celebrations.

VOTING IS COMPULSORY, YOUR VOTE IS SECRET
· · · · · · ·

Singapore has had thirteen general elections since independence in 1965. When the main opposition party, the Barisan Sosialis, walked out in 1966, the People's Action Party faced empty benches in Parliament. In 1968, the PAP took all seats when elections were held. This began a streak of one-party rule that was only broken in 1981, when an opposition candidate, Joshua Benjamin Jeyaratnam of the Workers' Party, beat Pang Kim Hin of the PAP. In 2020, history was made when ten candidates from the opposition Worker's Party, the most ever since 1965, were elected as Members of Parliament.

WATER, WATER EVERYWHERE
· · · · · · ·

Speaking of waterfalls, Singapore is home to several man-made ones. The first man-made waterfall, 30 metres high, opened at Jurong Bird Park in 1971. In 2012, a 35 metre tall waterfall at the Gardens by the Bay welcomed its first visitors. Located in an air-conditioned conservatory, the waterfall is a must-see part of the gardens' Cloud Forest. The latest indoor waterfall in Singapore is the HSBC Rain Vortex at Jewel Changi Airport. At 40 metres tall and pumping half a million litres of the water, it is a spectacular sight with water cascading from the roof to the basement of the building.

LOCAL FAVOURITES AND THEIR CALORIFIC VALUES

Chicken rice
618 kcal

Satay
(without peanut sauce)
10 sticks, 240 kcal

Laksa
587 kcal

**Nasi briyani,
with chicken**
880 kcal

**Roti prata, plain,
with curry gravy**
317 kcal

Nasi Lemak
279 kcal

Curry fish head
385 kcal

SPECIAL EDUCATION IN SINGAPORE

There are currently eighteen Special Education (SPED) schools in Singapore. Run by Social Service Organisations (SSO), these schools run programmes that cater to children from a range of ages and disability profiles. The first such centre in Singapore was the Trafalgar Home in 1947, which served children with leprosy. Schools for the visually handicapped and the blind were also set up in the 1950s. In 1962, the forerunner of the Movement for the Intellectually Disabled of Singapore (MINDS) was set up to attend to children with intellectual disabilities. In 1987, the first school to cater to children with multiple disabilities opened at Margaret Drive. Now known as the Rainbow Centre, it runs two schools that cater to children with autism and multiple disabilities.

HDB, NOT AS EASY AS 1-2-3

The Housing and Development Board (HDB) is Singapore's housing authority and a statutory board that plans and develops public housing. Its mission is to provide affordable homes of quality and value. Buyers can choose from a variety of flats. Do note that the term "room" in HDB-speak includes the living area, therefore a 3-room flat in fact has two bedrooms and a living room.

Studio apartments
Between 35 and 45 square metres

2-room flats
Approximately 45 square metres

3-room flats
Between 60 and 65 square metres

4-room flats
90 square metres

5-room flats
110 square metres

FROM RUBBISH TO NATURE

One of Singapore's 63 islands, Pulau Semakau, is home to Singapore's award-winning landfill. The landfill covers an area of 350 hectares (about 440 football fields), and has a capacity of 63 million cubic metres. To create the landfill, a 7-kilometre rock bund was built into the sea between Pulau Semakau and Pulau Sakeng, which was absorbed in the process. The landfill, which opened in April 1999, is the only working landfill in Singapore.

Pulau Semakau is also a nature-lover's paradise. Mangroves on its eastern shore, which were affected by the perimeter bund, were recovered and replanted. In July 2005, it was opened to for selected recreational activities such as guided walks, birdwatching, sport fishing and stargazing. Four plants listed as endangered in Singapore are found on the coastal and intertidal areas of Semakau. The Seashore Bat Lily (*Tacca leontopetaloides*) and the seagrass *Syringodium isoetifolium* are found only on the island.

BEFORE YOU CHOP DOWN THAT TREE...
. . . .

Singapore prides itself on being a city in a garden. No surprise then that it is an offence to chop down, without permission, any tree with a girth greater than 1 metre (3 feet) growing within a designated tree conservation area, or on any vacant land. Some mature trees, both inside and outside tree conservation areas, have also been designated as heritage trees and are protected by law. These trees have historical value and enhance the landscape.

In 2003, property management company DTZ, Debenham Tie Leung, learned the hard way that the law takes its trees very seriously. In 2002, the company cut down a tree with a girth measuring 3.4 metres (11.15 feet) because a building supervisor was concerned for the safety of the tenants in two of its nearby properties.

Unfortunately for DTZ, they had neglected to do their due diligence. The tree they had cut down was the *Hopea sangal* tree. It was in a tree conservation area, was more than 100 years old and was believed to be the last of its kind. DTZ was fined S$8,000 for illegally felling the tree, and the judge ordered them to pay S$76,035 to the state as compensation. Really smack on the wrist for a company that makes millions every year.

Source: *The Straits Times*, 7 Jul 2009

PHILOSOPHY – SINGAPORE STYLE
. . . .

Whenever something goes wrong, expect these words of assurances from fellow Singaporeans:

"WHAT TO DO?"

"Won't die, lah." = "You will survive this."
"Die? Die, lah!" = "Whatever will be will be."
"Ne'er mine, lah." = "It's fine."
"Like that, lah." = "That's life."
"What to do?" = "There's nothing that can be done about it."

A TROPICAL WASTELAND

In 2018, 7.7 million tonnes of waste was generated by Singaporeans.

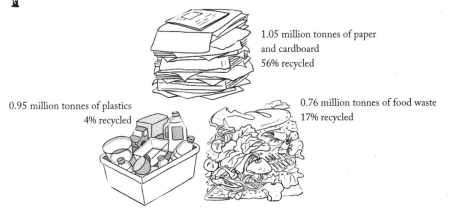

1.05 million tonnes of paper and cardboard
56% recycled

0.95 million tonnes of plastics
4% recycled

0.76 million tonnes of food waste
17% recycled

Source: National Environment Agency

WHAT DIGS!

The most extravagant grave in Singapore belongs to Ong Sam Leong (1857 - 1918) and was located at the now defunct Bukit Brown cemetery. A businessman, Ong supplied labour for the phosphate mines on Christmas Island and he also owned brickworks, sawmills and plantations. Sam Leong Road, off Jalan Besar, bears his name.

The tomb of Ong and his wife, covering 600 square metres, is a giant among the 100,000 tombs at Bukit Brown. It has all the traditional Chinese tomb features executed on a grand scale. The symbolic moat, which is little more than a groove in other tombs, is 15 metres (50 feet) long in Ong's grave. Besides the usual lion guardians, there are also statues of two Sikh watchmen, complete with rifles.

The huge tomb was "lost" for a few years as the old cemetery became neglected and overgrown with weeds. It was rediscovered only in 2006.

Source: *Discover Singapore*

HOME AWAY FROM HOME?

In a 2019 HSBC survey on expats about the best places to live and work, Singapore came in second, after maintaining its top spot since 2015. Switzerland pipped Singapore for the top spot. Some of the criteria used include - qualify of life, political stability, economic stability, ease of settling in, and work-life balance.

Rank	Location
1	Switzerland
2	Singapore
3	Canada
4	Spain
5	New Zealand
6	Australia
7	Turkey
8	Germany
9	United Arab Emirates
10	Vietnam

ORIGINS OF ROTI JOHN

Sometime in the 1960s, an Englishman asked a Malay hawker in Sembawang for a hamburger. As hamburgers were not commonly available, the ingenious hawker concocted a substitute. He spread minced mutton and slices of onion between slices of French loaf (baguette), dipped the creation in beaten egg, and fried it on a hot griddle. The name of the dish is attributed to this anonymous hawker, who was overheard saying, "*Silakan makan roti, John*" which means "Please eat this bread, John".

SINGAPORE MUSICALS
· · · · · · ·

Singaporeans are a practical lot, but they have been known to sing and dance on occasions. Here is a selection of "Made in Singapore" musicals:

- Beauty World (1988)
- Makan Place (1988)
- Fried Rice Paradise (1991)
- Kampong Amber (1994)
- Yum Sing! (1999)
- Corporate Animals (1995)
- Sing to the Dawn (1996)
- Snow.Wolf.Lake (1997)
- Chang and Eng (1997)
- Hotpants (1997)
- Sayang (2001)
- Forbidden City (2002)
- Dim Sum Dollies (2003)
- Pagoda Street (2005)
- Roses & Hello (2005)
- Lao Jiu (2005)
- The Snow Queen (2005)
- Oi! Sleeping Beauty! (2005)
- Blue Willow House (2006)
- No Regrets: A Tribute to Edith Piaf (2007)
- Shanghai Blues (2008)
- Sleepless Town (2009)
- A Singaporean in Paris (2010)
- Tropicana (2017)
- You are here (2021)

FRONT PAGE NEWS
· · · · · · ·

A sampling of the front-page advertisements on 15 July 1845, the date of the first issue of Singapore's longest-established English daily newspaper, *The Straits Times*:

"FOR SALE TWO Guzerat Milch Goats with three kids: all in excellent condition. Apply to the printer of this paper."	"A comfortable and conveniently situated House in High Street, suitable for a family; with out-house complete. Apply to the printer of this paper."	**"FOR SALE** A few boxes of fresh Japan Rice. Cursetjee & Co."

THE SINGAPOREAN DIET

· · · · · · ·

A report by the Singapore Food Agency revealed that Singaporeans consume a relatively healthy diet that comprises more fruits and vegetables than any other type of food. In 2018, an average Singaporean chomped down:

Vegetables
96 kg

Fruits
72 kg

Chicken
34 kg

Fish
15 kg

Pork
22 kg

Eggs
338 eggs

Beef
3 kg

Mutton
2 kg

WORLD'S FASTEST GROWING TREE
· · · · · · ·

A lbizia trees (*Falcataria moluccana*) are a non-native species that Singapore would like to get rid of. Found in East Malaysia and the Solomon Islands, the trees were first grown in the Singapore Botanic Gardens in the 1870s and have since proliferated. One experiment showed that an Albizia sapling could grow a whopping 10.7 metres (35 feet) in 13 months – or 2.6 centimetres (0.1 foot) a day – making it a candidate for the fastest-growing tree in the world. The tree is also a nuisance in other ways. Its wood is lightweight and "weedy" - it is neither strong nor durable and is of little economic value.

The Albizia has never featured as a wayside tree in Singapore's plans as a city in a garden. This is despite its beautiful, spreading canopy. It is seen as a hazard because of its tendency to shed branches and to fall over in storms. In 2007, Albizia trees were earmarked for the chop after one on a woman. A tender document related to a Tree Conservation Area (TCA) specifies that "(a)ny trees within the TCA are to be retained except for the Albizia trees".

Source: *Trees of Our Garden City*

OLD BUILDINGS, NEW USES
· · · · · · ·

St James Power Station	Dyson global headquarters
Istana Kampong Glam	Malay Heritage Centre
Wan Qing Yuan	Sun Yat Sen Memorial Hall
Tao Nan School	Peranakan Museum
Supreme Court/City Hall	National Art Gallery
Old Ford Factory	Exhibition Gallery - Surviving the Japanese Occupation
Fullerton Building	Fullerton Hotel
Convent of the Holy Infant Jesus	CHIJMES entertainment complex

AFFAIRS OF THE HEART
· · · · · · ·

Cardiovascular disease is the biggest cause of death in Singapore, responsible for 32.4 per cent of all deaths. A survey showed that 70 per cent of Singaporeans know that chest pains and breathlessness are symptoms of a heart attack.

However, this does not mean that the rate of death by cardiac arrest is about to fall anytime soon. One fifth of respondents (21.8 per cent) would rather lie down and rest than call an ambulance or a doctor, or even a family member.

The reasons for neglecting chest pains by percentage of respondents:

Worried about treatment cost .... 51.5 %
Fearful of diagnosis .... 32.2 %
Afraid of surgery .... 30.2 %
Worried about loss of salary during recovery 19.6 %
Worried about side effects .... 18.3 %

Source: *The Straits Times*, 22 Jan 2010

RECIPE FOR "MADRAS CHUNAM"
· · · · · · ·

Madras chunam was a low-cost plaster used in the construction of some of our heritage buildings like the St Andrew's Cathedral. It was also used to make the ornamental façades of some old shophouses.

Ingredients
egg-white
sugar
coconut husk
shell lime

Method
Mix well with water, then apply to walls. When dry, polish smooth with stones.

FOOD ON THE MOVE
· · · · · · ·

S ingapore hawker food is loved by locals, tourists and TV food show hosts alike.
Here is an account of what the street food scene was like in 1860s Singapore:

> There is probably no city in the world with such a motley crowd of
> itinerant vendors of wares, fruits, cakes, vegetables. There are Malays,
> generally with fruit; Chinamen with a mixture of all sorts, and *Kling* with
> cakes and different kinds of nuts. Malays and Chinamen always use the
> shoulder-stick, having equally-balanced loads suspended at either end;
> the *Klings*, on the contrary, carry their wares on the head on trays. The
> travelling cookshops of the Chinese are probably the most extraordinary
> of the things that are carried about in this way. They are suspended on
> one of the common shoulder-sticks, and consist of a box on one side
> and a basket on the other; the former containing a fire and small copper
> cauldron for soup, the latter loaded with rice, vermicelli, cakes, jellies,
> and condiments; and though I have never tasted any of their dishes, I
> have been assured that those they serve up at a moment's notice are most
> savoury, and that their sweets are delicious. Three cents will purchase a
> substantial meal of three or four dishes from these itinerant restaurateurs.

- John Cameron, *Tropical Possessions in Malayan India*

TELOK AYER STREET
· · · · · · ·

D id you know that Telok Ayer Street, which parallels Amoy Street, was the
coastline of Singapore until 1878? Until the late 19th century, Telok Ayer Street
was one of the main thoroughfares in Singapore. There used to be ten places of
worship catering to different religions and beliefs along Telok Ayer Street. Thian
Hock Keng Temple (built 1841) was one of the most popular, and not far from it was
the Al-Abrar Mosque (built 1827). The Nagore Durgha Shrine (built 1828) was on
the corner of Telok Ayer Street and Boon Tat Street. Today, these historic places of
worship are a testament to Telok Ayer's multicultural past.

SINGAPORE'S FIRST BOTANIC GARDENS
· · · · · · ·

The Singapore Botanic Gardens in Tanglin, designated as a UNESCO World Heritage Site, was set up in 1859. However, did you know that there was a botanic gardens established earlier than this?

The first Botanic Gardens was initiated by Sir Stamford Raffles, Singapore's founder and a keen naturalist. It was located on the slopes of what was then called Government Hill (now known as Fort Canning Hill). The purpose of the gardens was to determine if there was any money to be made from cultivating crops such as nutmeg, cloves and cocoa. Sadly, it proved too costly to upkeep and was closed in 1829.

PUBLIC HOUSING AT ITS FASTEST
· · · · · · ·

The Housing and Development Board (HDB) was set up by the government in 1960 to address the chronic housing shortage in Singapore. Over the years the cumulative total number of flats built has grown by leaps and bounds. There are now over a million HDB flats in Singapore.

1963	21,000
1965	53,777
1970	117,225
1980	358,568
1990	667,575
2000	924,488
2008	990,573

Sources: Housing Development Board; Singapore Department of Statistics

SNAKES ALIVE
· · · · · · ·

Even a highly built-up place like Singapore has its fair share of wildlife sightings, including snakes. Here are some you would want to steer clear of:

Mildly venomous

- Big-eye Green Whip Snake or Malayan Whip Snake
- Crab-eating Water Snake
- Cantor's Water Snake
- Dog-faced Water Snake
- Dog-toothed Cat Snake
- Gold-ringed Cat Snake or Mangrove Snake
- Jasper Cat Snake
- Keel-bellied Whip Snake
- Oriental Whip Snake
- Painted Mock Viper
- Paradise Gliding Snake or Paradise Tree Snake
- Puff-faced Water Snake
- Twin-barred Gliding Snake or Twin-barred Tree Snake
- Yellow-lipped Water Snake or Gerard's Water Snake

Venomous

- Amphibious Sea Snake or Yellow-lipped Sea Kriat
- Banded Malayan Coral Snake
- Banded Krait
- Blue Malayan Coral Snake
- Blue-necked Keelback
- King Cobra
- Equatorial Spitting Cobra or Black Spitting Cobra
- Mangrove Pit Viper or Shore Pit Viper
- Wagler's Pit Viper

Non-Venomous

- The Reticulated Python lacks poison, but the constrictor is one of the largest snakes in the world

Source: *Wild Animals of Singapore*

LIST OF APPROVED PETS IN SINGAPORE

- Rabbits
- Guinea pigs
- Hamsters
- Gerbils
- Mice
- Chinchillas
- Red-eared sliders (a kind of terrapin)
- Birds (some require papers)
- Fish (some require papers)
- Land hermit crabs (*Coenobita rugosus*)
- Green tree frogs (*Litoria caerulea*)
- Malayan box turtles (some require papers); and of course, most species of dogs and cats.

POPULATION BOOM

Year	Total Population
1824	10,683
1901	250,000+
1947	557,745
1957	938,144
1970	2,074,000
1980	2,413,000
1990	3,047,000
2000	4,027,000
2007	4,588,000
2008	4,839,000
2010	5,076,000
2015	5,535,000
2019	5,638,700

Source: Singapore Department of Statistics

VERY IMPORTANT ORCHIDS

The National Orchid Garden at the Singapore Botanic Gardens houses up to 60,000 orchid plants comprising 400 species and more than 2,000 hybrids. The most interesting ones are the orchid hybrids that have been named after VIPs as a diplomatic gesture to honour important state visitors. There are more than 100 of these "Very Important Orchids" and the first was the Aranthera Anne Black, named in 1956 after Lady Black, wife of Sir Robert Brown Black, the former Governor of Singapore. Other Very Important Orchids include the Dendrobium Memoria Princess Diana, the Vandaenopsis Nelson Mandela and the Renaglottis Ricky Martin.

KIPLING QUOTE ON RAFFLES HOTEL

British poet, Rudyard Kipling (1865–1936) said this about the Raffles Hotel in the 1880s:

> **"Providence conducted me along a beach, in full view of five miles of shipping – five solid miles of masts and funnels – to a place called Raffles Hotel, where the food is as excellent as the rooms are bad. Let the traveller take note. Feed at Raffles and sleep at the Hotel de l'Europe."**

The hotel went on to use it loosely for its advertisements.

> **"Feed at Raffles, where the food is excellent."**

SODA FOR SALE

Soda water was first advertised for sale on 31 August 1836 at the Singapore Dispensary. The price was $1.50 per dozen, not including the bottles.

SCARRED FOR LIFE
· · · · · ·

Caning has been part of Singapore criminal law since 1824. The offender to be caned is tied naked to a trestle so that he is bent over, with buttocks exposed. The lower back and kidney areas are protected by padding. The rattan cane, which is 1.2 metres long and 1.3 centimetres wide, is soaked overnight, to stop it from splitting or from shearing the skin. It is treated with antiseptic before the offender's buttocks are hit, and a medical officer is on hand to stop the caning if necessary. Today, caning is mandatory for more than 40 offences, among them rape, robbery, drug-trafficking, possession of offensive weapons, vandalism and illegal overstaying. For rioting, extortion, living off the immoral earnings of another, manslaughter, causing hurt and certain road traffic offences, caning is discretionary.

Sources: *Singapore the Encyclopedia*; *The Straits Times*

SINGAPORE'S POSTER GIRL – AH MENG
· · · · · ·

Arguably Singapore's most famous tourism icon, Ah Meng, a Sumatran orangutan, was kept in illegal captivity before being rescued by a veterinarian in 1971 and rehoused at the Singapore zoo. Ah Meng went on to a stellar career as a poster girl for the zoo and a Singapore tourism icon.

In 1982, the zoo introduced its most signature programme – "Breakfast with Ah Meng". This raised awareness about the Sumatran orangutan and the protection of its natural habitats. Ah Meng passed on in 2008 at a ripe of age of 47, leaving behind five children and a clutch of grandchildren. 4,000 visitors attended a memorial service held in her honour on 10 February 2008.

CHINESE NEW YEAR TRADITIONS

Chinese New Year is the most important festival celebrated by the Chinese. Lasting fifteen days, it is also known as the Lunar New Year or Spring Festival. Though there are many traditional practices associated with this festival, some are no longer practised or have been updated to suit a more contemporary setting.

- **New Year's Eve:** After the reunion dinner, leave the lights on until 12.30 am. Children stay up late as it is believed that this practice will ensure that their parents have a long life.

- **New Year Day 1:** Don't sweep the floor or you will sweep away your good luck. Visit your relatives. Make sure you have red packets to give out if you are married.

- **Day 2:** If shops plan to open on the third day, they must open for a short while on the second day, symbolically to announce the reopening of business the next day.

- **Day 3:** The third day is known as "chi kou", directly translated as "red mouth". "Chi kou" means "the God of Blazing's Wrath" and it is generally accepted that it is not a good day to socialise with relatives and friends. Avoid visiting others.

- **Day 4:** Taoists pray for their gods to descend from heaven back to earth. They burn paper offerings, printed with sedan chairs, to fetch them back to the mortal world.

- **Day 5:** At noon, Taoists welcome the gods back. People used to light up firecrackers, in an attempt to get the God of Wealth's attention, thus ensuring his favour and good fortune for the New Year.

- **Day 7:** Man's birthday, the day when everyone turns a year older. Restaurants are full, and everyone eats *yusheng* for good luck, as well as noodles for longevity.

- **Day 8:** At midnight, pray to the King of Heaven for long life, good fortune and health. Among the offerings are two branches of sugar cane to represent all the generations in the family, and a bunch of bananas to represent fertility. Teochews offer only vegetarian spread, while Hokkiens offer only meat, especially a pig's head.

- **Day 9:** Trousers should not be washed or it will insult the King of Heaven.

- **Day 15 (*Chap Go Maey*):** The family gathers for dinner to celebrate the closing of New Year. Business people then go to temples (the Waterloo Street temple is popular) to get two red packets, each filled with 20 cents. These are put in the till of their shops to bring in revenue. The favour must be returned before the end of the year with four red packets.

ONE FOR THE ROAD

Under the Liquor Control (Supply and Consumption) Act which came into force on 1 April 2015:

- Drinking is banned in all public places from 10.30 pm to 7 am.

- Retail shops are also not allowed to sell takeaway alcohol from 10.30 pm to 7 am.

- Liquor Control Zones have been demarcated in Little India and Geylang. In these zones, public drinking is banned from 7 am on Saturday to 7 am on Monday. It also applies from 7 pm on the eve of a public holiday to 7 am after the holiday. The sale of takeaway alcohol is prohibited during these times.

After a review, the sale of non-beverage alcohol products such as rum and raisin ice cream was permitted in 2019. While you can't have a pint of beer in the park after 10:30 pm, a pint of ice cream is certainly an option!

SINGAPORE COIN SPECIFICATIONS

1 Cent
- Image: Singapore's national flower, Vanda Miss Joaquim, a special hybrid of orchid known for its sturdiness.
- Weight: 1.24 g
- Diameter: 15.90 mm
- Thickness: 1.10 mm
- Edge: Plain
- Metal: Copper-plated zinc

5 Cents
- Image: The Fruit Salad Plant (*Monstera deliciosa*), a heavy foliage climber which grows slowly. The leaves on young plants are uncut, mature leaves are heavy, leathery and dark green.
- Weight: 1.56 g
- Diameter: 16.75 mm
- Thickness: 1.22 mm
- Edge: Milled
- Metal: Aluminium Bronze

10 Cents
- Image: The Star Jasmine (*Jasminum multiflorum*), a handsome slender climber. The plants bears, at frequent intervals, large numbers of pure white, star-like flowers.
- Weight: 2.60 g
- Diameter: 18.50 mm
- Thickness: 1.38 mm
- Edge: Milled
- Metal: Cupro-nickel

20 Cents
- Image: The Powder-puff Plant (*Calliandra surinamensis*), a medium-sized shrub with beautiful leaves divided into leaflets. Its flowers are arranged in hemispherical heads.
- Weight: 4.50 g
- Diameter: 21.36 mm
- Thickness: 1.72 mm
- Edge: Milled
- Metal: Cupro-nickel

50 Cents
- Image: The Yellow Allamanda (*Allamanda cathartica*), a vigorous vine that can grow up to 15 metres (50 feet) long. It bears large, velvety, bright yellow flowers shaped like trumpets.
- Weight: 7.29 g
- Diameter: 24.66 mm
- Thickness: 2.06 mm
- Edge: Those issued before 1989 have milled edges, while those

issued from 1989 onward have plain edges with the inscription "REPUBLIC OF SINGAPORE" and the lion symbol.

- Metal: Cupro-nickel

$1

- Image: The Periwinkle (*Lochera rosea*), a small shrub with single or branched stems. The flowers are produced in the uppermost leaf axils and contrast beautifully with the glossy, dark green foliage of the plant.
- Weight: 6.30 g
- Diameter: 22.40 mm
- Thickness: 2.40 mm
- Edge: Milled and bearing the inscription "REPUBLIC OF SINGAPORE" and the lion symbol.
- Metal: Aluminium Bronze

Source: Monetary Authority of Singapore

HAPPY BIRTHDAY, SINGAPORE!

Some trivia about the annual National Day Parade:

- The day is nearly always blessed with good weather. There were only five instances in 54 years (as of 2019) when the parade was held in the rain – 1968, 1975, 1977, 1980 and 2008.
- The 1969 parade not only celebrated Singapore's 4th birthday, but also the 150th anniversary of its founding by Sir Stamford Raffles. It was also the only time there was a special guest at the parade – Princess Alexandra from the UK. For the very first time, fanfare trumpets were featured in the military band, playing the national anthems of both the UK and Singapore.

Source: Wikipedia

FILMED IN SINGAPORE

H ollywood and other "foreign" film studios have been using Singapore as an exotic locale in film productions since the 1920s. Here are some examples:

1928
Across to Singapore
Directed by: William Nigh
Starring: Joan Crawford, Ramon Navarro

1931
The Road to Singapore
Directed by: Alfred E Green
Starring: William Powell, Doris Kenyon

1940
The Letter
Directed by: William Wyler
Starring: Bette Davis

1940
Road to Singapore
Directed by: Victor Schertzinger
Starring: Bing Crosby, Bob Hope

1947
Singapore
Directed by: Johannes Brahm
Starring: Ava Gardner, Fred MacMurray

1954
World for Ransom
Directed by: Robert Aldrich
Starring: Dan Duryea, Gene Lockhart

1979
Saint Jack
Directed by: Peter Bogdanovich
Starring: Ben Gazzara, Denholm Elliott

1999
Rogue Trader
Directed by: James Deardon
Starring: Ewan McGregor

Source: *Singapore the Encyclopedia*

FROM 3% TO 4% TO 7%

I ndirect taxation in the form of a goods and services tax (GST) was introduced to Singapore on 1 April 1994. Singaporeans had to adjust to paying a 3% tax on their purchases. The GST is applied across the board on all goods and services, and collected at every stage of the production chain. In 2003, the GST hiked to 4% and in 2007, it went up further to 7%. Subsidies, grants and rebates are routinely disbursed to reduce the impact of GST, especially on lower-income households.

BEST LOCAL TRAINING GROUND FOR F1 DRIVERS
· · · · · · ·

Though we might not have the near-180° hairpin turns worthy of Lombard Street in San Francisco, or the Fairmont Hotel Hairpin of the Circuit de Monaco, most local drivers claim the stretch of South Buona Vista Road from the National University Hospital to Pasir Panjang Road on the west coast to be challenging. Known in local dialect as "99-bends", it is a narrow two-lane carriageway, with a cliff face on one side and a steep drop on the other. It boasts of no less than five sharp turns over a road distance of 800 metres to boot.

GIVING VOICE TO THE DEAD
· · · · · · ·

The late Professor Chao Tzee Cheng (1934–2000) was Singapore's first and most famous forensic pathologist. His original ambition was to be a surgeon, but a serious road accident weakened his right arm and changed his life forever. Despite being right-handed, he successfully willed himself to use his left hand. He became a forensic pathologist because, as he used to joke, "I can't kill anyone!" He went on to become internationally respected for his unrelenting pursuit of justice and forensic expertise.

THE MARINA 10
· · · · · · ·

Smooth coated otters, once thought to be extinct, have made a comeback in Singapore. Capable swimmers and navigators, they are believed to have swum across the Straits of Johore and made their homes here. You are likely to spot them in places such as Bishan Park, the Kallang River estuary and Marina Bay. The last group is so famous that they have been dubbed "the Marina 10". There are currently about seventy otters in Singapore and it is illegal to capture or trap them.

FLUSH WITH SOCIETIES

There are more than 7,000 registered societies in Singapore, formed between 1980 and 2010, representing diverse hobbies, passions, beliefs and professional interests. Here is a handful of the more interesting ones:

- **Bliss and Wisdom Society**
  a Buddhist association
- **COLLECTIVE mayhem**
  a multi-disciplinary art group
- **Hetero Poetry Club**
  a Chinese poetry forum
- **Singapore Chinese Riddle Club**
- **The Headache Society of Singapore**
  a chapter of the International Headache Society advocating the management of headache in a scientific and ethical manner, and helping headache sufferers relieve their condition

- **Chihuahua Lover Club**
- **Python User Group (Singapore)**
  an association for users of Python, a computer programming language
- **Guppy Club**
- **Society for Anti-Aging Medicine (Singapore)**
  a medical society in educating doctors and the public on anti-ageing issues
- **House Rabbit Society (Singapore)**
  a society dedicated to rabbit welfare and awareness
- **Rope Skipping (Singapore)**

WE LOVE OUR COFFEE

1. As of 2019, there are 146 Starbucks and 47 Coffee Bean and Tea Leaf outlets in Singapore.

2. Singapore was the third country outside North America to have Starbucks cafés and the first Starbucks café opened on 14 December 1996 at Liat Towers along Orchard Road.

3. Indie coffee joints, some boasting single origin coffee beans or house roasts, have become popular in Singapore. One of the forerunners in this market segment is Forty Hands, located in the hip Tiong Bahru enclave.

LIGHTHOUSES OF SINGAPORE
· · · · · · ·

- **Horsburgh Lighthouse,** situated on Pedra Banca Island ("White Rock" in Portuguese), is the oldest amongst the five lighthouses in Singapore. Built in 1851 at a cost of 23,665.57 Spanish dollars, it was named after Captain James Horsburgh, a distinguished hydrographer of the East India Company.

- **Raffles Lighthouse** was built in 1855 on Pulau Satumu ("One Tree Island" in Malay). Named after Sir Stamford Raffles, the foundation of the lighthouse was laid in 1854 by the Governor of the Straits Settlements, William J. Butterworth.

- **Sultan Shoal Lighthouse** is situated in Singapore's Western Anchorage, about 5.46 km from Singapore island. It was built in 1895.

- **Pulau Pisang Lighthouse** was built in 1914 on an island off the western coast of Johore in the Staits of Melaka. As part of an arrangement between the Sultan of Johor and the Governor of the Straits Settlements in 1900, Singapore manages and operates this lighthouse. Pulau Pisang's sovereignty, however, resides with Malaysia.

Source: Maritime Port Authority of Singapore

Horsburgh Lighthouse

BORDER CROSSINGS
· · · · · · ·

S ingapore is connected to mainland Malaysia by a causeway and a bridge. The causeway is among the world's busiest border crossings, with over 300,000 people and 145,000 vehicles crossing it each day.

PICK YOUR THORNY FRUIT
· · · · · · ·

Mon Thong (meaning "golden pillow"): fleshiest of all varieties of durian with pale-coloured flesh and a mild taste. One of the most popular varieties because it can be harvested long before ripening and travels well.

Chan Nee (meaning "gibbon"): less fleshy than the Mon Thong, it has a slightly more pungent taste and smell than its Thai counterpart.

Ganja: extremely sweet yellow flesh that counterbalances the pungent smell. The name is probably a reference to the sugar high that will follow.

D4: this one resembles vanilla custard because of its very pale yellow colour. It is fleshy and tastes bitter.

D11: smooth and creamy with a sweet aftertaste. This is one of the less pungent varieties.

D15: smooth and very creamy with a hint of bitterness. This variety is so fleshy that it is hard to find the seed sometimes. Too rich for some palates.

D24: one of the more expensive varieties, this one has a bittersweet taste. With small seeds and plenty of dark yellow flesh, this is good value for money.

XO: one of the most expensive varieties but tread carefully. It has a bitter taste and an alcoholic aftertaste.

Hong Xia (meaning "red prawn"): so named because its flesh is the colour of a cooked prawn, this one offers a softer texture than other varieties. The flesh is reddish-orange and thin, with an aroma that hits you before the fruit is opened.

101: this is a crowd-pleaser, with its plump reddish flesh and sweetness.

Hor Lor (meaning "water gourd"): not only is its shape different, its soft flesh is drier than other varieties and it tastes bitter. Very strong smell.

Mao Shan Wang (meaning "mountain cat king"): with flesh that is firm on the outside and creamy on the inside, it has a bitter first taste which ends on a sweet note. Considered the best and most satisfying of all durian varieties, it combines all the best characteristics of the durian.

HAPPY DAYS ARE HERE AGAIN!
· · · · · · ·

The Sikh bands that were once used at Chinese funeral processions were made up of retired members of the Singapore Police Force band. Upon retirement, they formed small brass bands that played selections from the repertoire they were familiar with. They were soon sought after to play at Chinese funeral processions, which required loud music to "send off" the dead in a rousing fashion and to keep lurking evil spirits at bay. And "Happy Days Are Here Again!" was a familiar refrain at these events as was Elgar's "Land of Hope and Glory".

Source: *Notes Across the Years – Anecdotes from a Musical Life*

MONUMENTS AT THE ESPLANADE PARK
· · · · · ·

Indian National Army Monument – This memorial, inscribed with the Urdu words *ittefaq*, *itmad* and *kurbani* which mean "unity", "faith" and "sacrifice", was dedicated to the Unknown Soldier of the Indian National Army (INA). Built in the final months of the Japanese Occupation (1942 - 1945), it was demolished by the British soon after. The National Heritage Board has marked the site with a plaque.

The Cenotaph – The inscription "They died that we might live" gives the Cenotaph an air of solemnity. It was first dedicated to 124 British soldiers born or resident in Singapore who gave their lives in World War I. A second dedication was made for those who died in World War II. Designed by architect Denis Santry, the foundation stone of the Cenotaph was laid on 15 November 1920 by Sir Lawrence Guillemard, the Governor of Singapore.

Tan Kim Seng Fountain – Businessman, Chinese leader and philanthropist Tan Kim Seng was a Malaccan immigrant who came to Singapore in the 1820s. Unveiled in 1882, the Tan Kim Seng Fountain commemorates his generous contribution of S$13,000, made in 1857, towards setting up the city's first reservoir and waterworks.

Source: *Singapore's 100 Historic Places*

ICONIC PILLAR BOXES

The red pillar box outside the Singapore Philatelic Museum is the only one of its kind in Singapore in use today. A relic of British colonial rule, this pillar box was originally adorned with the Royal Cipher on its door. Upon Singapore's independence in 1965, the royal ciphers were removed.

The first pillar box, made of cast iron and weighing about 400 kg, was introduced in 1873. In 1971, they were replaced by rectangular post boxes. On 19 August 1995, the pillar box outside the Singapore Philatelic Museum was officially re-commissioned.

A similar pillar box resides at the Fullerton Hotel. Shipped from the UK, it serves as a reminder of the building's former role as the General Post Office. The Royal Cipher of Queen Elizabeth II, the reigning British monarch, adorns its door. Although you can drop a letter off, it will never get delivered as it is not operational.

Sources: Singapore Philatelic Museum; The Fullerton Hotel Singapore

SPEAKERS OF PARLIAMENT

Singapore has had eight Speakers of Parliament since independence. They are:

- A.P. Rajah (1964 - 1966)
- P. Coomaraswamy (1966 - 1970)
- Dr. Yeoh Ghim Seng (1970 - 1989)
- Tan Soo Khoon (1989 - 2002)
- Abdullah Tarmugi (2002 - 2011)
- Michael Palmer (2011 - 2012)
- Halimah Yacob (2013 - 2017)
- Tan Chuan-Jin (2017 - incumbent)

A IS FOR...
· · · · · · ·

In order to improve and maintain good personal and food hygiene, all licensed retail food establishments are assessed annually by the National Environment Agency and graded. These are:

A (Excellent)   – a score of 85 per cent or higher
B (Good)   – a score of 70 to 84 per cent
C (Average)   – a score of 50 to 69 per cent
D (Below Average) – a score of 40 to 49 per cent

However, as it is thought that the improvement in hygiene would have taken some flavour out from the cuisine, some Singaporeans have made an alternative interpretation of the grading system based on the quality of the food served:

A (Atrocious)
B (Bad)
C (Can make it)
D (Delicious)

This grading system, which was introduced in 1997, is slated to be replaced in late 2020 with one that focuses on track record and consistency.

Source: National Environment Agency

OUR HISTORIC MILESTONES
· · · · · · ·

All roads in Singapore used to converge on the General Post Office (GPO) at the Fullerton Building. Designated 'point zero', the GPO was the datum from where road distances were measured. From here, milestones were laid along major roads and thoroughfares. The milestones provided people with a reference point as they plied their trade, visited their friends or made reports about tiger sightings. In the 1970s, the milestones were phased out after Singapore went metric. Old habits die hard though as some older Singaporeans still use these milestone to refer to their old haunts.

SIGNS THAT YOU HAVE BECOME A TRUE SINGAPOREAN
..

1. You pat MRT and bus seats to cool them before you sit down.

2. Your wedding photos include shots of you dressed up like Louis XIV, Michael Jackson, or Leonardo DiCaprio and Kate Winslet in *Titanic*.

3. You won't raise your voice to protest government policies you disagree with, but you'll raise your fists to whack someone over Hello Kitty.

4. You don't know three quarters of the people attending your wedding.

5. You get married to take advantage of public housing subsidies and the Baby Bonus.

6. You feel the urge to add the suffix "-polis" to everything: Biopolis, Airtropolis, Fusionopolis, Entrepolis, etc.

7. Your children have a rudimentary knowledge of Tagalog or Bahasa Indonesia.

8. You wear winter clothes indoors and summer clothes outdoors.

9. You will gladly spend $50,000 on a car, but will go to great lengths to save a few dollars on ERP charges.

10. Pork floss and mayonnaise on bread is a completely natural combination to you.

11. You have started referring to colleagues from overseas as "foreign talent".

12. At the dinner table, you are always discussing where better versions of whatever you are having can be found.

13. You pronounce the letter R as "ah-rer" and the letter H as "haytch".

14. No matter how old you are, you keep associating people with their secondary schools. (Alternative: No matter how old you are, you secretly need to know how people fared in their PSLE, O levels and A levels.)

15. You 'chope' a seat or a table by placing a packet of tissue paper on the chair.

16. You are very forthright with your criticisms of the "Gahmen" (government), unless there is a chance they might actually hear you.

17. You diligently track the whereabouts of your favourite hawkers, ie you know that the famous Tiong Bahru bao is now in Jurong, the famous Outram char kuay teow is now in Hong Lim Centre and the famous Lau Hock Kien Hokkien mee from the old Lau Pa Sat is now at Beach Road.

18. You complain about everything and anything under the sun that can be complained about.

Sources: www.talkingcock.com; *NDP Book 2003: Things That Make Us Singaporean*

TILL DEATH DO US PART?

People get married in churches, but who gets married in a Chinese temple? The dead, it seems. Home of the City God Cheng Huang, the patron of departed souls, the Seng Wong Beo Temple has made a name for itself conducting ghost marriages.

Ghost marriages are carried out when the dead appear to their families in dreams asking his family to help him find a bride, usually another deceased person. The bride's family might experience a similar visitation. Ideally, both sets of parents eventually find each other and a match is made.

For those who died as singles, the temple helpfully provides a matchmaking service. The couple is introduced to each other through rites at the ancestral altar. After a match is struck, a wedding takes place. Effigies of the bride and groom, paper gifts and offerings are burnt after the ritual is completed.

Source: *The Sunday Times*, 8 Sep 2002

JOSEPH BALESTIER
· · · · · ·

B alestier Road was named after Joseph Balestier, the first American consul to Singapore. He developed the area in 1834 when he leased 1,000 acres of land for a sugar cane plantation and named it Balestier Plain. He was married to Maria Revere, the daughter of the famous American bell-maker and patriot, Paul Revere, maker of the Liberty Bell in Philadelphia. In 1843, Marie Revere donated a Revere bell to the Saint Andrew's Cathedral - the only Revere bell outside the USA. It is now part of the National Museum of Singapore's collection.

Source: National Heritage Board

ROAD TO MANDALAY
· · · · · ·

O ne interesting feature of the Balestier area is the large number of Burma-themed roads. It is believed that the suggestion to name roads after Burmese towns and kingdoms came from an old and respected Burmese resident in the area. Others speculate that it could be because of the proximity to the Burmese temple's original location at Kinta Road or they could even have been named after various British conquests in Burma. Some examples are:

Akyab Road – named after a port in Burma
Bassein Road – named after a river town
Bhamo Road – named after a Burmese town
Irrawaddy Road – named after the Irrawaddy river
Mandalay Road – named after the royal capital of Burma from 1860 to 1885
Martaban Road – road was named in 1929 to continue the Burmese theme in the area
Pegu Road – named after a river town
Prome Road – named after one the oldest cities which was a commercial town and port in 1952
Rangoon Road – named after the administrative capital of British Burma

Source: National Heritage Board

THE ICE HOUSE
· · · · · · ·

O pened in 1854, Whampoa's Ice House at present day Clarke Quay was Singapore's first such facility. It sold imported ice hewn from the frozen lakes of New England at a time when refrigeration did not exist. The man behind this bold venture was Whampoa Hoo Ah Kay, a prominent businessman and public figure. Though a brilliant idea, the icea business failed because there was little demand. The Ice House was eventually sold to a bank, and the building occupied by a rubber company. It was eventually demolished but a replica was built near its original site.

Source: National Heritage Board

MOST COMMON CONDITIONS OF HOSPITALISATION
· · · · · · ·

	2008	2018
Total No. of Discharges ('000)	442.2	611.9
% of Total Discharges		
Accidents, poisoning & violence	9.3	8.6
Cancer	5.7	5.8
Ischaemic heart disease	3.6	3.1
Pneumonia	2.6	3.2
Obstetric complications affecting foetus or newborn	2.4	n.a.
Chronic obstructive lung disease	2.3	2.0
Other heart diseases	2.3	2.5
Cerebrovascular disease (including stroke)	2.1	2.0
Intestinal infectious disease	1.8	2.7
Infections of skin and subcutaneous tissue	2.0	2.3
Diabetes mellitus		2.1

Source: Ministry of Health

BRIDGING THE GAP
· · · · · ·

There are altogether 12 named bridges over the Singapore River. They are, in order of increasing distance from the mouth of the river:

- Anderson Bridge (1910)
- Cavenagh Bridge (1869)
- Elgin Bridge (1929)
- Coleman Bridge (1840)
- Read Bridge (1889)
- Ord Bridge (1886)
- Clemenceau Bridge (1940)
- Alkaff Bridge (1997)
- Pulau Saigon Bridge (1891)
- Robertson Bridge (1998)
- Jiak Kim Bridge (1999)
- Kim Seng Bridge (1885)

As part of urban redevelopment and rejuvenation, Cavenagh, Read, Ord, Alkaff, Robertson and Jiak Kim bridges have now been pedestrianised.

CROWDED GRAVE
· · · · · ·

The most heavily populated cemetery spot in Singapore has got to be the Japanese Cemetery at Chuan Hoe Road. Founded in 1891 as a burial ground for Japanese karayuki-san, or prostitutes, it is also home to the remains of Japanese civilians, members of the Japanese military killed in the Second World War, as well as convicted war criminals who were executed after the war crimes trials in Singapore. In 1947, it stopped accepting burials and in 1987, became a memorial park. The Japanese Association in Singapore is responsible for maintaining it.

IT'S TOUGH BEING A SINGAPORE GIRL
· · · · · · ·

If you have ever wondered why, after a few drinks on-board, you cannot tell one immaculately groomed Singapore Girl apart from another, it is because the girls have to observe Singapore Airlines' meticulous grooming and make-up code religiously. Here are some of the rules they have to follow:

1. Hair colour is either black or dyed dark brown; no highlights are allowed. Stewardesses with long hair have to coil their hair into buns or French twists.

2. No fanciful, dangling earrings; only simple studs or pearls are allowed. No chains or necklaces are allowed, but simple bracelets and rings can be worn. Watches must be small and simple.

3. A spare kebaya uniform must be brought for every flight, even short one-hour flights.

4. Safety shoes or covered sandals must be worn during take-off and landing. At other times, stewardesses should wear batik slippers.

5. Eyebrows must be elegantly shaped, and not be drawn-on or tattooed. Eye shadow must be of the colour prescribed by the company – either blue or brown, depending on skin tone.

6. Lipstick colour must be among the few shades of bright red prescribed by the company. Pink or plum colours are not allowed.

7. Finger and toe nails have to be groomed and painted in the bright red colour prescribed by the company. Nails should not be chipped.

CAVENAGH BRIDGE
· · · · · · ·

Completed in 1869, Cavenagh Bridge no longer bears coolies and cargoes but still serves as a pedestrain bridge. A police notice that prohibits all cattle and horses from using the bridge is a reminder of its past.

A SELECTION OF CLUBS

1. Singapore Cricket Club
2. Chinese Weekly Entertainment Club
3. Ee Hoe Hean Club
4. Ceylon Sports Club
5. Singapore Khalsa Association
6. Chinese Swimming Club
7. Singapore Turf Club

QUEENSTOWN FIRST

The Queenstown housing estate in Singapore was the country's first satellite town, which saw the first public housing flats, the first branch of the National Library, the first neighbourhood shopping centre and the first sports complex. Before its development as a housing estate, Queenstown was a large swampy valley with a channel running across it in a southeastern direction. During this time, the area was inhabited by a small farming community who cultivated fruits and vegetables, and kept pigs and chickens.

ISLAND LIFE

Singapore has lost more than 95 per cent of its original forest cover. Only 24 square kilometres of it remain. Despite this shrinkage, it is estimated to be home to more than 40,000 wild plant and animal species – and that is before including micro-organisms such as bacteria, fungi, protozoa and microalgae. Amazingly, there are even a number of species that are unique to Singapore. One of these was the "Singapore orchid" (*Dendrobium laciniosum*). It was so rare that only a single example of this flower was collected in 1891. Sadly, it is now extinct.

Source: *Singapore Biodiversity*

ACRONYM HEAVEN

A cronyms abound in Singapore and here are a handful of the more common ones you will encounter:

HDB	Housing Development Board	ERP	Electronic Road Pricing
PAP	People's Action Party	MRT	Mass Rapid Transit
PUB	Public Utilities Board	MOH	Ministry of Health
MOE	Ministry of Education	NLB	National Library Board
MAS	Monetary Authority of Singapore	ROM	Registry of Marriages
LTA	Land Transport Authority	SPH	Singapore Press Holdings
CPF	Central Provident Fund	PA	People's Association
MOH	Ministry of Health	CC	Community Club
SGH	Singapore General Hospital	NTUC	National Trades Union Congress
SFA	Singapore Food Agency	NEA	National Environmental Agency

GRAVE MATTERS

I n land-scarce Singapore, space for both the living and the dead is limited. For those who do not wish to be cremated, burial is an option. In 1998, the government announced the New Burial Policy (NBP) to cap the burial period at 15 years. After that, the graves will be exhumed (or enbloc-ed, as property obsessed Singaporeans would put it) and the remains cremated. They will then be placed in a columbarium or reburied, in accordance to one's religious requirements. Ever innovative, the government introduced concrete burial crypts in 2007 to use limited burial land more efficiently. Today, Choa Chu Kang Cemetery in the far west of Singapore is the only one still open for burials.

Sources: National Environment Agency

SINGAPORE FLAG

O n 3 December 1959, the Singapore flag was introduced to the people. It is the nation's most visible symbol and is raised daily in government buildings and schools. The Singapore flag consists of two equal horizontal sections, red above white. In the upper left of the red section, there is a white crescent moon, and five white stars which form a circle. Red symbolises universal brotherhood and the equality of man, while white signifies pervading and everlasting purity and virtue. The crescent moon represents a rising young nation. The five stars stand for the nation's ideals of democracy, peace, progress, justice and equality.

The use of the Singapore flag is governed by the Singapore Arms and Flag and National Anthem (Amendment) Rules 2007. The flag must be treated with respect and dignity at all times. It must not be allowed to touch the ground, displayed beneath any other flag or emblem and inappropriately dipped in salute to any person or object.

IS THE MUSEUM HAUNTED?

A Cambridge-educated medical scientist, Carl A Gibson-Hill arrived in Singapore in December 1941. He spent the Japanese Occupation interned in Changi Prison as a prisoner of war. In 1947, he was appointed Curator of Zoology of the Raffles Museum (today's National Museum of Singapore) and was the made museum director. In August 1963, Gibson-Hill died unexpectedly, just days before he stepped down from his post.

The academic's death, the circumstances of which were shrouded in secrecy, sparked much public interest and speculation. Some suggested that he had committed suicide. Officially, *The Straits Times* reported that he died from an overdose of sleeping pills.

Since then, there have been numerous ghost sightings at the museum. Night watchmen in particular have confirmed the presence of a nocturnal visitor resembling Gibson-Hill in both appearance and manner. The newer museum attendants, who have never met Gibson-Hill, are quite certain that they have seen something glide through the darkened halls at night, ascending the old wrought-iron spiral staircase that connects the museum's second floor with the eaves above ...

Source: *National Museum of Singapore Guide*

FARMS IN SINGAPORE
. . . .

Agriculture in Singapore exists in the form of six agrotechnology parks, equipped with the necessary farming infrastructure. These are located at Lim Chu Kang, Murai, Sungei Tengah, Nee Soon, Mandai and Loyang. As of 2015, there are 217 modern farms that cater to the production of livestock, eggs, milk, aquarium and edible fish, vegetables, fruits, orchids, ornamental and aquatic plants, as well as the breeding of birds and dogs.

Activities	Number of Farms	Total Area (hectares)
Fisheries		
Aquarium fish	64	139
Edible fish and shrimp	9	34
Livestock		
Poultry	3	48
Others	9	26
Horticulture		
Vegetables	57	114
Orchids/Ornamentals	75	247
	217	608

Source: Agri-Food and Veterinary Authority of Singapore

ASSIGNED, STAMPED, DELIVERED
. . . .

The first stamps to be used in Singapore were from British-ruled India. When the colony faced a shortage of postage stamps between 1855 and 1886, the Postmaster cut the existing stock of stamps diagonally into two, thus doubling the quantity. This was the first and last time that stamps in Singapore were bisected.

LAKSA WARS
· · · · · · ·

In a country known as a food paradise, competition between hawkers is intense, sometimes leading to "food wars". Often, stalls claim to be "famous" or "original" or "the best" version of a Singaporean dish. One such battle for supremacy centred around three versions of laksa, all located within a stone's throw of each other along East Coast Road. Laksa is a dish of rice noodles served in a rich and spicy soup, with accompaniments such as shrimp, cockles, fish cake, bean sprouts, dried tofu, and chilli paste. This food war led to verbal skirmishes between the three stalls as they claimed and vied to be top dog in this competition. The irony - laksa can be found all over the island and though they may not be the best, the most famous or the original, they suffice to scratch the laksa craving most of the time.

LOCAL JARGON
· · · · · · ·

Here are some common Malay place terms found in Singapore, and their meanings in English:

Malay term	English meaning
Bukit (eg Bukit Timah)	hill
Jalan (eg Jalan Kayu)	road, street, walk
Lorong (eg Lorong Mambong)	alley
Taman (eg Taman Jurong)	garden, park
Tanah (eg Tanah Merah)	earth, land, soil
Tanjong (eg Tanjong Pagar)	cape
Telok (eg Telok Ayer)	bay

STARTING THE DAY RIGHT
· · · · · · ·

In multicultural Singapore, breakfast is a smorgasbord of flavours that leaves one spoilt for choice. Here are some of the most well-loved traditional foods to start your day with.

- **Kaya toast** – toast served with kaya (coconut jam) and a slab of butter. To complete the meal, soft-boiled eggs drizzled with soy sauce and pepper are often served.

- **Chwee kueh** – steamed rice cakes, topped with bits of diced preserved turnips, and served with sambal chilli on the side.

- **Chee cheong fun** – thin sheets of rice dough are rolled up, stuffed with dried shrimp and radish, and then steamed. It is sometimes served with **rice porridge** containing slices of fish, shredded chicken, cuttlefish strips, century eggs and boiled or fried peanuts.

- **Roti prata** – a fluffy and crispy pastry fried on a hot iron griddle and served with spicy curry gravy. It is also a popular choice for late-night supper. Who says you can't have breakfast twice a day?

- **Thosai or appom** – lacy rice-and-lentil flour pancakes cooked with a little oil on a hot griddle. They are accompanied by condiments such as coconut chutney, potato curry and sambar (spicy vegetable stew).

- **Putu mayam** – steamed pancakes of rice vermicelli served with orange colored palm sugar and coconut or with a curry gravy.

- **Nasi lemak** – Rice (or nasi) cooked in coconut milk with pandan leaves. It is served with fried egg, cucumber slices and fried anchovies, with sambal chilli on the side.

- **Mee Siam** – thin rice vermicelli is served in a mildly spicy and sour gravy, topped with a boiled egg, sliced fish cake and tau kwa (a deep fried tofu).

- **Lontong** – steamed rice cakes served in a rich vegetable gravy with a topping of hardboiled egg.

- **Mee Rebus** – yellow egg noodles served in a spicy gravy thickened with sweet potato and garnished with dried shrimp, bean sprouts and bean curd.

ART FOR EVERYONE
· · · · · · ·

It is little known that Singapore has been a rich repository of public art since the 19th century. Here is a selection of public artworks in the Civic District:

Title: **Elephant**
Artist: Unknown
Year: 1871
Location: The Arts House, side entrance facing the Padang

Title: **Sir Stamford Raffles**
Artist: Thomas Woolner
Year: 1887
Location: In front of Victoria Theatre and Concert Hall

Title: **Allegory of Justice**
Artist: Cavalieri Rodolfo Nolli
Year: 1939
Location: Roof Pediment of the former Supreme Court

Title: **Merlion**
Artist: Lim Nang Seng
Year: 1972
Location: Merlion Park

Title: **Deva**
Artist: Emery Lin
Year: 1986
Location: In front of the Pan Pacific Hotel

Title: **Abundance III**
Artist: Sun Yu-Li
Year: 1993
Location: intersection of Raffles Boulevard and Temasek Boulevard

Title: **Six Brushstrokes**
Artist: Roy Lichtenstein
Year: 1997
Location: Roy Lichtenstein Sculpture Plaza, Millenia Singapore

Title: **Seed Series**
Artist: Han Sai Por
Year: 1998
Location: Esplanade Waterfront

Title: **First Generation**
Artist: Chong Fah Cheong
Year: 2000
Location: Along the Singapore River, next to The Fullerton Hotel

Title: **Fishing by the River**
Artist: Chern Lian Shan
Year: 2005
Location: Along the Singapore River, in front of The Riverwalk

OLYMPIAN ACHIEVEMENTS
· · · · · ·

Tiny Singapore is not without her Olympians. On 9th September 1960, at the Palazzetto Dello Sport in Rome, Tan Howe Liang put Singapore on the world map when he lifted a record 380 kg in the lightweight (67.5 kg) category to beat 33 rivals (except Russia's Viktor Busheuv) for the silver medal. Tan is also the only Singaporean who has won a medal at all the major international games – the Olympics, Commonwealth Games, Asian Games and the Southeast Asian Peninsular (SEAP) Games, taking all Golds except for the Olympics. He was also the first weightlifter in history to be awarded the International Weightlifting Federation (national honour) Gold Award in 1984. Tan's sterling achievements were surpassed by Joseph Schooling, who took home Singapore's first Olympic gold medal in the 100m men's butterfly in a record time of 50.39 seconds at the 2016 Rio de Janerio Olympics.

Source: www.sportsmuseum.com.sg

OPEN FOR BUSINESS
· · · · · ·

According to a study, Singapore is the world's most globally connected economy. The Globalisation Index 2009, by Ernst and Young and the Economist Intelligence Unit showed Singapore beating Hong Kong, Ireland and Belgium as the most open economy, based on five criteria:

1. Openness to trade
2. Movement of capital
3. Exchange of technology and ideas
4. Openness to labour
5. Cultural integration

However, being number one in movement of goods and services relative to total output also means being open to big hits during a global recession, with the Republic suffering a 9.5 per cent year-on-year contraction in the first quarter of 2009.

LOCAL MALAY PROVERBS
· · · · · · ·

Proverb	Literal Translation	Meaning
Ada udang di balik batu.	There is a shrimp behind the stone.	There is a hidden motive behind an act.
Rambut sama hitam, hati lain-lain.	Same hair colour (black in this case), but different heart.	Everybody has a different way of thinking.
Memang lidah tak bertulang.	The tongue indeed has no bone.	To describe a person who makes unreliable promises.
Sepandai-pandai tupai melompat, akhirnya jatuh ke tanah jua.	No matter how well a squirrel can jump, eventually it will fall.	No matter how smart a person is, eventually they will make a mistake.
Sudah jatuh ditimpa tangga.	After falling off the ladder, the ladder falls on you.	After one bad thing, another follows.
Bagaikan kacang lupakan kulit.	Like the peanut forgetting its shell.	A person who forgets/ denies his roots.

THE WORLD'S HIGHEST POPULATION DENSITIES
· · · · · · ·

As of 2019, these ten countries have the world's highest population densities (people per square kilometres).

1. Monaco: **21650.3**
2. Macau **21419.6**
3. Singapore: **8291.9**
4. Malta: **1376.2**
5. Bahrain: **2169.4**
6. Bangladesh: **2,637**
7. Maldives: **1769.8**
8. Barbados: **667.5**
9. Mauritius: **625.5**
10. Nauru: **537.8**

THE GREAT SINGAPORE STOPOVER
· · · · · · ·

S ingapore is part of the East Asian-Australian flyway, the annual route taken by migratory birds as they fly from the colder to warmer climes. In the summer, they breed in the Arctic Circle, and as winter begins, they fly south, some touching down as far away as New Zealand.

During the annual migratory season from September to March, as many as 60 different species can be spotted in a single day in places such as Sungei Buloh and Chek Jawa. Around 19 per cent of migratory bird species, such as the Chinese Egret and the Masked Finfoot, are threatened or near-threatened species, which means that the maintenance of their stopover destinations, such as Singapore, is critical.

A single flight ranges from 4,000 kilometres to 11,000 kilometres, non-stop. Some birds travel more than 20,000 kilometres in a year. Weighing as little as 15 grams, they are designed by nature to do so.

THE LEGEND OF BUKIT MERAH
· · · · · ·

B ukit Merah literally means "red hill" in Malay. Malay legend has it that fishermen were frequently attacked by swordfish. A boy who lived on the hill advised the Sultan to build a fence of banana tree trunks in the sea. When the swordfish came in with the tides, they got stuck in the banana trunks. The Sultan, however, saw the clever boy as a threat and ordered his soldiers to kill him. The boy's blood flowed down the hill and stained the soil red, giving rise to the name.

WHAT IS A VOID DECK?
· · · · · ·

U nique to Singapore, the term "void deck" refers to the free space on the ground floor of public housing apartment blocks. Usually furnished with tables (with a checker board incorporated into the design), benches and bicycle racks, the void deck is a communal space. Weddings, funerals, exercise and *taichi* sessions, all-day chess and checkers games, romantic trysts, late night studying, just hanging out … it all happens at the void deck.

FOOD FADS
. . . .

What do Rotiboy buns, bubble tea, Portuguese egg tarts, Beard Papa cream puffs, apple strudel, Miki Ojisan No Mise cheesecake, doughnuts and cupcakes have in common?

All are delicious and sweet, and were, at one time or another in the past decade, major food fads in Singapore. Snaking queues were seen everywhere they were sold, tens of thousands of items were bought each day and a kind of crazy frenzy took hold of normally restrained Singaporeans. In 2019, Singaporeans took to mala hotpot and salted egg potato chips with a vengeance.

CHINESE-FRENCH-INDIAN-ITALIAN-MALAY-JAPANESE?
. . . .

In January 2010, the Ministry of Home Affairs announced that a child of mixed heritage will be allowed to "take on a double-barrelled race", meaning the race of both parents can be recorded on the child's registration papers. With an increasing diversity in the demographics of the country, stemming from an inflow of migrants and Singaporeans marrying foreigners, mixed marriages are fast becoming a trend.

In the past, a child with mixed race parents could only be classified as "Indian" for example, always taking after the father's race. Now a child with an Indian father and Chinese mother can have their mixed race reflected as "Indian-Chinese".

Complications could arise with both parents having double-barrelled races, British-Malay and Chinese-Indian, for instance. Professor Ho Peng Kee, Minister of Home Affairs, said parents will have to choose any two of the four races to declare for their child. However, he urged parents not to rush to register their child's race at birth as changes can be made any time before the child turns 15.

Sources: *The Straits Times*; AsiaOne

VERY SINGAPOREAN NO-NOS

1. Point your finger at the moon and the Moon Goddess will cut off your ear.

2. Don't whistle at night. You will attract "entities".

3. If you take a photograph of someone who is asleep, their soul will be captured and trapped within the image.

4. If you draw on the face of someone who is sleeping, their soul will not be able to recognise them and return to their body.

5. It is said that the face of a prisoner about to be hanged is covered with a black hood so that he cannot see those witnessing the execution. This ensures that his vengeful soul will not come back to haunt those who had watched him die.

6. If you pare a red apple with a knife while staring into a mirror, in the dark, at midnight, you will see the face of your future spouse. Caveat - the peel has to be in one continuous piece.

I LOVE THE DENTIST

In 1929, when Singapore's first dental clinic opened in Outram Road, it became such a novelty that people literally arrived in lorry loads. It cost 30 cents for a child's tooth to be extracted and $1 for an adult. Due to high demand, the clinic moved to a two-storey building in the same neighbourhood in 1938.

Source: National Heritage Board

THE JURY IS OUT

Singapore abolished all jury trials in its judicial system in 1969. A decade earlier, in 1959, jury trials had been abolished for all except capital offences that carried the death penalty.

THE OLDEST TEMPLE
· · · · · ·

Thian Hock Keng Temple on Telok Ayer Street is the oldest Chinese temple in Singapore. Built in 1821 by immigrants from Fujian province, it was where those who had arrived safely in Singapore came to offer their thanks and offerings of joss sticks to the goddess Ma Zu, the protector of seafarers and navigators. With generous donations from leading Hokkien merchants such as Tan Tock Seng, Thian Hock Keng was transformed from a humble prayer house into an ornate and lavish temple in 1842. Some 30,000 Spanish dollars, a fortune in those days, was spent on this undertaking that was built in traditional Southern Chinese style by skilled craftsmen from China. No expense was spared as all building material, including its ironwood pillars, were imported from China.

Here are five fun facts about the temple:

- In 1998, when the temple was being restored, workers found a scroll in one of the roof beams. It was written by the Qing emperor Guang Xu, who pronounced blessings on the Chinese community in Singapore.

- The low granite barrier across the entrance serves two purposes. The first was to keep seawater out during high tide, because this was once a seaside temple. The second purpose is spiritual. To get over the barrier, you have to bend your body in a "bowing" posture. Symbolically, this shows respect to the deities within.

- At the ceiling of the right wing of the temple, there is a statue of a man who looks as if he is lifting a beam. The man looks Indian, and the statue is there as a reminder and a gesture of appreciation to the Indian migrants from nearby Chulia Street who helped build the temple.

- Not a single nail was used in its construction.

- The patron deity, Ma Zu, was shipped from Amoy (now Xiamen), Fujian province, and arrived in Singapore in April 1840

Gazetted as a national monument by the Preservation of Monuments Board in 1973, the temple has been extensively restored to its former glory over the years.

DURIANS ON THE BAY

Officially opened on 12 October 2002, the Esplanade – Theatres on the Bay (sometimes referred to as "the Durian" due to its spiky facade) is a prominent landmark on the waterfront. A performing arts centre, it incorporates a theatre, concert hall, studios and dining and retail spaces. It features aluminium sunshades that shield the interior from the sun, but which also allow unobstructed views of the city.

CLOSEST SOUND-A-LIKES

I grew up in the music environment of the '50s in which the greatest compliment you could earn was that you sounded exactly like someone else. So the local neighbourhood (in my case, Pasir Panjang) was full of Elvis Presleys, Paul Ankas, Frank Sinatras, Pat Boones, Johnny Rays and Nat King Coles, each with his own following. Competition was friendly, so if there were two Pat Boones, one would be the Pat Boone of Pasir Panjang (5th Mile) and the other the Pat Boone of Pasir Panjang (6th Mile). Generally the Pat Boone types attracted docile followers but the Elvis types tended to attract more local gangsters so that arguments over who did the most convincing version of Jailhouse Rock often ended in coffeeshop brawls.

– Singapore-born blues artiste Siva Choy, writing on the music scene in the 1950s and '60s, "Those Sixties Sound-a-Likes" for The Ultimate Tribute Concert 2002 Souvenir Programme

THE GOVERNMENT ALWAYS WINS

With the opening of two casinos in Singapore, the government put in measures in the form of a casino levy to curb problem gambling. A daily entry levy of $150 is charged if a Singapore citizen or permanent resident wants to enter the casino. For regulars, an annual entry levy of $3,000 is available. Upon payment, the patron can stay in the casino for a twenty-four hour period. Entry into the casino is through designated lanes. Overstaying in a casino is an offence. Between 2010 and 2018, $1.3 billion in casino levies were collected by the government. The deck is indeed stacked against the gambler in Singapore.

CHASING THE DREAM

While Singaporeans aren't usually big risk-takers, they are certainly more than willing to try their luck gambling. In 2017, Singaporeans spent a total of S$7.2 billion on 4D, Toto and Sports Betting. The biggest Toto win of S$13,943,682 on 19 February 2016 was pocketed by two individuals, who had placed their bets in Marina Bay Sands and Ubi Avenue respectively. The biggest 4-D win in history was claimed by a man in his 40s in September 2005. The S$14-million prize, however, was estimated to have cost him bets between S$4,667 and S$7,000. It is unsurprising then that Singaporeans will go to great lengths to get lucky numbers. These include:

- Taking down registration numbers of accident vehicles
- Travelling to remote parts of Singapore and Malaysia to pray to deities renowned for revealing winning digits
- Turning up at funerals and murder sites to pray and look for lucky numbers
- Consulting mediums and seeking divine intervention
- Visiting websites for advice on strategic combinations

Source: Singapore Institute of Management

COME SEE WHAT WE'RE LOOKING AT

Singapore's top-rated visitors attractions are:

- Botanic Gardens
- Chinatown
- Singapore Zoo and Night Safari
- Gardens by the Bay
- Raffles Hotel
- Marina Bay Sands and Art Science Museum
- Sentosa and Cable Car
- Singapore Flyer

Source: Department of Statistics Singapore

ROADWORTHY NEWS

- **Oldest Road** – Serangoon Road is possibly Singapore's oldest road, marked on ancient maps as "The Road Through the Island".

- **Longest Road** – Yio Chu Kang Road is the longest road in Singapore, excluding expressways, measuring about 14 kilometres.

- **Shortest Road** – The shortest road in Singapore is Tua Kong Green, measuring only 25 metres long.

- **Road Length** – In terms of lane-kilometres, Singapore is home to 9,293 kilometres of roads. These include 1,107 lane-kilometres of expressways. Roads occupy around 12% of Singapore's total land area.

Source: www.streetdirectory.com

BIRTHQUAKE

The record number of births earned the Kandang Kerbau Hospital consecutive entries in the Guinness Book of Records from the 1950s to the 1970s as the world's largest and busiest maternity hospital. The 1975 edition of the Guinness Book of Records revealed: "The largest maternity hospital in the world is the Kandang Kerbau Government Maternity Hospital in Singapore. It has 239 midwives, 151 beds for gynaecological cases, 388 maternity beds and an output of 31,255 babies in 1969 compared with the record 'birthquake' of 39,856 babies (more then 109 per day) in 1966."

Source: National Heritage Board

AND THE RIVER FLOWS...

The Singapore River snakes its way from River Valley Road to the coast for a distance of approximately 3.8 kilometres. The Kallang River, which is 10 kilometres long, takes the accolade of being Singapore's longest river.

THE WAY TO FLY
· · · · · · ·

C hangi International Airport, the pride of many Singaporeans, commenced operations with only one terminal in July 1981. Today, it has four main terminals (and a fifth under construction), serving over 100 international airlines flying to some 380 destinations in 100 countries and territories. The airport handles about 7,400 arrivals and departures every week and over 65.6 million passengers a year.

Over the years Changi Airport has won over 616 awards, making it one of the most internationally recognised airports in the world.

Number of times Changi Airport has received the following accolades:

- World's Best Airport (Skytrax): **10** (2000, 2006, 2010, 2013 - 2019)
- Best Airport in World: **27** (1992 - 2019)
- Best Airport in the Asia-Pacific : **10** (2010 - 2019)

Source: Singapore Changi Airport

RELIGIOUS COMPOSITION OF THE MAIN ETHNIC GROUPS
· · · · · · ·

I n 2015, the major faiths in Singapore were:

1. Buddhism/Taoism 43.2%

2. Christianity 18.8%

3. Islam 14%

4. Hinduism 5%

5. No religion 18.5%

6. Other religions 0.6%

23% of those aged 15 to 24 reported having no religious affiliation compared to 14.6% of those aged 55 and over.

HAUNTED PLACES IN SINGAPORE

- **Fairy Point Hill, Selarang Camp and Changi Prison**
  The entire Changi peninsula was an internment camp for around 15,000 British and Australian troops taken prisoner by the Japanese after the fall of Singapore in 1942.

- **Old Ford Motor Factory**
  Lieutenant-General A.E. Percival, Commander of the British forces in Singapore, surrendered to General Yamashita of the Imperial Japanese Army here in 1942. There have been reports of strange lights and sounds coming from the building since.

- **Mount Pleasant Cemetery along Thomson Road**
  This place is commonly believed to be frequented by *pontianaks*.

- **Nee Soon Camp White House**
  According to sources, people often hear ghostly sounds.

- **Old Changi Hospital**
  An old military command quarters for the British before World War II, the hospital was later converted into a military hospital. Rumour has it that spirits can be seen wandering around the hospital grounds.

- **Pasir Ris Red House**
  The stone lions outside the house are said to move, turning their heads or making roaring sounds as someone passes by. The building has a long history of deaths and murders. Many unnatural sightings have also been reported here.

- **Woody Lodge**
  Woody Lodge was a home for the mentally ill. It appears that many lived here until they passed on. It is believed that the souls of the mentally deranged tend to remain earth-bound after death, and so the place is rumoured to be haunted by many spirits.

Disclaimer: Unfortunately we could not fully verify the information above.

NO LONGER JUST A MASTER OF THE SEA

In 2008, Singapore made it big on the silver screen when home-grown actor, Ng Chin Han was cast in Christopher Nolan's production, *The Dark Knight*. Ng landed himself a role portraying Lau, a Hong Kong mogul in cahoots with the crime syndicate from Gotham City. Ng, who started out in a local 1994 television drama *Masters of the Sea*, has gone on to star alongside Hollywood A-listers in films such as Captain America: Winter Soldier, Independence Day and Skyscraper.

THE GREAT SINGAPORE WORKOUT

The Great Singapore Workout was launched when then Prime Minister Goh Chok Tong flagged off and led a 3-kilometre walk-and-jog session from the National Stadium to the Padang on 3 October 1993. This was followed by a 15-minute exercise session done by a crowd of 26,107, which entered the Guinness Book of World Records for the "largest mass aerobic session held at one location."

Source: National Library Board Infopedia Talk

KAMPONG LORONG BUANGKOK

Located off Lorong Buangkok in Yio Chu Kang, Kampong Lorong Buangkok, or Kampong Selak Kain in Malay, is the last remaining kampong (village) in Singapore with 28 households and a multi-racial population of about 200. The low-lying land was reclaimed from a swamp and is extremely flood-prone, hence the name Selak Kain, literally meaning "hitching up one's sarong".

Source: *Singapore the Encyclopedia*

SINGLISH IN THE DICTIONARY

Singlish, a Singaporean variety of English that mixes English with Mandarin, Malay and even Tamil expressions, has two entries – lah and sinseh – in the online version of the Oxford English Dictionary, among its 60 million entries. Embarrassingly, this came just days before Singapore launched a campaign discouraging the use of Singlish.

The popular Singlish expression "lah" has been defined as "a particle used with various kinds of pitch to convey the mood and attitude of the speaker", as in "Come with us, lah" to emphasise persuasion, and "Wrong, lah", demonstrating annoyance.

"Sinseh" refers to the traditional Chinese physician or herbalist.

Source: *South China Morning Post*, 14 Mar 2000

I NOW PRONOUNCE YOU...

There have been some strange cases brought to the Singapore courts, but this annulment request in 1991 was the first of its kind. A Malaysian woman had the shock of her life when she was unable to consummate the marriage with her husband. Her macho-looking husband was, to her shock and horror, once a woman. The marriage was annulled in court as husband and wife were considered "both of the female sex".

PUT SOMETHING ON, WILL YOU?

Under the Miscellaneous Offences Act, it is illegal to wander naked (outside of your bathroom of course) around your home in Singapore. You may be fined up to $2,000 and given a three-month jail sentence if you are convicted of appearing and exposing yourself to public view in a private place.

SINGAPORE FIRSTS
· ·

Bar Top Dancing

On 31 July 2003, the first legal bar top dancing took place simultaneously in three bars: Coyote Ugly, Devils Bar and 31 The Bar. Up until 2003, dancing in nightspots was only permitted in designated dancing areas.

Anti-Spitting Campaign

The first national campaigns were launched in 1958, shortly after the People's Action Party took power in the City Council elections. The first campaign launched was the anti-spitting campaign in August that year, to check the unhygienic social habit prevalent then.

Van Houten Chocolate Factory

The first chocolate factory in Singapore opened in Tanglin Halt in March 1965. The factory produced cocoa and chocolate products to meet local and overseas demands. The cocoa beans used in the factory came from Malaysia (Sabah and Terengganu) and Ghana, and the packaging was manufactured locally.

F1 Night Race

The inaugural 2008 Formula 1 Singtel Singapore Grand Prix achieved double firsts. It was the first night race in F1 history and the first street race in Asia. It was held on 28 September 2008.

Christmas Light-up

The first Christmas light-up, organised by the Singapore Tourism Promotion Board (now Singapore Tourism Board), took place on 13 December 1983. The illuminative decorations stretched the length of Orchard Road, starting from Ming Court Hotel (now Orchard Parade Hotel) to outside the Istana. Since then, the Orchard Road Christmas light-up has become an annual highlight.

The First Strike

The first major strike was staged by rickshaw pullers in 1897. The first rickshaws arrived in Singapore in 1880 and this mode of transport quickly became popular. By 1897, there were over 20,000 pullers. The protest culminated when the government attempted to regulate the trade through the Rickshaw Ordinance, forcing pullers to strike.

In-Vitro Birth

Singapore's (and Asia's) first test-tube baby or baby born by in-vitro fertilisation (IVF), was born in 1983.

Source: *Book of Singapore's Firsts*

HOME TO MANY

Singapore may be a highly urbanised country, but it is also rich in biodiversity. It is home to:

2,900 species of plants

360 species of birds

250 species of hard corals

Source: "A Lively and Liveable Singapore" in *Strategies for Sustainable Growth* published by the Ministry for the Environment and Water Resources and Ministry of National Development, 2009

THE VIEW FROM OUTSIDE

Quotes from various visitors to Singapore:

"Singapore – a vision of green hills and red dust, a sickly odour of pepper, cocoa, nut-oil, and drains."

— Harry de Windt, Explorer and Travel Writer
"From Pekin to Calais by Land",
The Travellers' Dictionary of Quotation, 1889

"The first impression of Singapore as we slide in is that it is about the greenest place that I have ever seen. It is like entering Dartmouth on a muggy August afternoon."

– Harold Nicolson, diplomat, politician and author,
Journey to Java, 1957

"That modern apology for a Romantic Eastern Port."

– Paul Mark Scott, "India, A Post-Forsterian View",
Lecture to the Royal Society of Literature, 1968

"Singapore … possesses a mingled allure of the rapacious, the aggressive, the repellent and the extraordinary that any true pilgrim would relish… Flat, steamy, thickly humid, the island lies there in its hot seas, fringed with mangrove swamps, and from the air it looks like it always did, a slightly desperate place that ought to be uninhabited. It looks like an invented place, and so of course, it is."

– Jan Morris, Travel Writer,
"The City-State", *Travels*, 1976

"I find it well laid-out, very orderly with a kind of antiseptic atmosphere."

- Nobel Prize-winning Poet, Playwright and Writer Wole Soyinka,
The Straits Times, 10 Nov 2009

HOW TO ORDER YOUR COFFEE (AND TEA)

At *kopitiams*, tea and coffee are usually ordered with unique modifiers or a shorthand that indicate how you want your brew made.

- Kopi: Coffee with condensed milk
- Kopi-O: Coffee with sugar only ("O" = black in Hokkien)
- Kopi-C: Coffee with evaporated milk and sugar
- Kopi-gau: Strong coffee ("gau" = strong brew in Hokkien)
- Kopi-po: Weak coffee ("po" = weak brew in Hokkien)
- Kopi-C-kosong: Coffee with evaporated milk and no sugar ("kosong" = empty/none in Malay)
- Kopi-O-kosong: Coffee (black) without sugar or milk
- Kopi-O-kosong-gau: A strong coffee without sugar or milk
- Kopi-bing, Kopi-peng or Kopi-ice: Coffee with milk, sugar and ice ("bing" or "peng" = ice cold or with ice cubes)
- Kopi-siu-dai: Coffee with less condensed milk ("siu-dai" = less sugar)
- Kopi-gah-dai: Coffee with extra condensed milk ("gah-dai" = more sugar)
- Kopi-di-lo: All coffee, no water (i.e. extra thick coffee)

To order other hot beverages, just substitute "kopi" with "teh" or "milo".

WILD NIGHTS

Chinatown was not always the tourist attraction it is now, replete with good food and cheap souvenirs. In 1887, it was known as *Bu Ye Tian* – the place of nightless days – due to the countless brothels and opium and gambling dens that were found there.

THAIPUSAM
· · · · · · ·

Thaipusam is a Hindu festival celebrated every year in January or February, according to the full moon in the Tamil calendar. The word is derived from "Thai" meaning "10th" and "pusam" meaning "when the moon is at its brightest". Dedicated to the Hindu God, Lord Subramaniam son of Lord Siva, also known as Lord Murugan, the deity of youth, power and virtue, this festival is a time for repentance for devotees with celebrations carried out mainly at the temple. Devotees prepare themselves spiritually with extensive prayer and fasting before performing acts of penance or thanksgiving through carrying a *kavadi* (burden) from one temple to another. The *kavadi* carriers often pierce sharp skewers through their tongues, cheeks and bodies as a form of self-mortification. They congregate at the temples early in the morning, with their families, friends and well-wishers, to participate in the procession. The procession in Singapore starts at the Sri Srinivasa Perumal Temple at Serangoon Road, goes down Orchard Road and ends at the Sri Thandayuthapani Temple at Tank Road, commonly known as the Murugan Temple or Chettiar's Temple. Offerings include fruits, flowers and pots of milk. This Hindu festival commemorates the feats of Lord Subramaniam reflecting triumph over evil forces.

SINGAPORE TIGERS
· · · · · · ·

Wild tigers were found in Singapore not that long ago around Bukit Timah, Choa Chu Kang and Pulau Ubin. Tigers were first reported in *The Singapore Chronicle* on 8 September 1831. They became a man-eating menace when large areas of forest were cleared for roads and plantations. Tiger hunts, which came with rewards, were common and led to the demise of the tiger. The last wild tiger was killed in 1932.

MONOPOLY, UNIQUELY SINGAPORE
· · · · · ·

C ontrary to the belief that Monopoly, Singapore style, equals "whatever you do, you'll get fined or thrown in jail", the board game has been a regular favourite in Singapore for decades. This particular edition, Monopoly – Uniquely Singapore was introduced as part of the country's "Uniquely Singapore" tourism campaign. The key difference between this and the Monopoly – Singapore edition is that instead of street names as real estate for purchase, the new board features clusters like the tourist attraction cluster, including the Singapore Zoo and Jurong Bird Park; the shopping cluster, including Marina Bay and Orchard Road; and the arts and entertainment cluster, including Victoria Concert Hall and the Esplanade. The game also introduces two new tokens of local flavour – the Kucinta cat and the trishaw.

WORDS TO LIVE BY - SINGAPOREAN SCHOOL MOTTOS
· · · · · ·

- Anglo-Chinese School.............................The Best Is Yet To Be

- Cedar Girls' Secondary............................Honesty, Perseverance, Courtesy

- Catholic High School..............................Care, Honesty, Service (in Chinese)

- Convent of the Holy Infant Jesus............Simple in Virtue, Steadfast in Duty

- Gan Eng Seng School............................. Onward

- National University of Singapor High School of Mathematics and Science..........
  Experiment. Explore. Excel.

- St Joseph's Institution..............................*Ora et Labora* (Pray and Work)

- Tanjong Katong Girls' School.................*Moribus Modestus* (Demure and Resolute)

- Tao Nan School.....................................Sincerity and Perseverance

- Victoria School......................................*Nil Sine Labore* (Nothing Without Labour)

- Yusof Ishak Secondary School...............*Ilmu Suluh Hidup* (Knowledge is the
  Light of Life)

SIZING UP THE SLING
. . .

"Cheap fruit cocktail. Over-sweetened cough medicine." That's what two visitors to the Long Bar at Raffles Hotel thought when they sampled the Singapore Sling in April 2010. In response to their letters to *The Straits Times* forum, the newspaper went in search of the best Singapore Sling, which is now sold at many different bars. The taste-tester was none other than Albert Yam, the great-grandnephew of the late Sling creator.

Ta.Ke, Studio M Hotel
Price: $21.20   Rating: **4.5/5**
Comments: "… you can taste the essence of the Sling's main ingredient…
If the original recipe is used, this would be the most innovative Singapore
Sling in terms of preparation …"

Loof, Odeon Towers
Price: $20.00   Rating: **4/5**
"… sweetness just about right … looks the part …"

Singapore Sling Boutique Bar, Clarke Quay
Price: $20.10   Rating: **3.5/5**
"… lacks the robust flavours of one that is made fresh."

No. 5, Emerald Hill Road
Price: $14.00   Rating: **3.5/5**
"… rather bitter aftertaste …"

Introbar, Swissotel The Stamford
Price: $11.77 (Happy Hour price from 3 pm to midnight)   Rating: **3.5/5**
"… quite sweet but you can still taste the gin …"

Alley Bar, Emerald Hill Road
Price: $12.23   Rating: **2.5/5**
"… very sweet … somewhat watered-down version …"

Long Bar, Raffles Hotel

Price $29.45 Rating: **NA**

"… This is not the Singapore Sling … can't be rated as it tastes nothing like the original recipe my relatives taught me … far too sweet … leaves an artificial aftertaste …"

Source: *The Sunday Times*, 9 May 2010

A FINE SELECTION OF OFFENCES ON THE MRT

Offence	Maximum penalty
Throwing missiles	$5,000
Bringing dangerous goods onboard	$5,000
Leaving motor vehicles on railway premises	$5,000
Spitting, littering or soiling	$5,000
Smoking	$1,000
Failure to pay fares	$1,000
Non-compliance with instructions	$500
Refusing to leave railway premises	$500
Causing nuisance	$500
Entering a train when it is full	$500
Failure to hand in lost property	$500

Source: Land Transport Authority

CITY DAY

D id you know that Singapore once had a City Day? On 22 September 1951, it was officially declared a City of the British Commonwealth, by proclamation of a Royal Charter issued by King George VI.

An estimated 300,000 people came for the celebrations, the largest crowd the city had ever seen. Held at the Padang and elsewhere around the island, it involved a military parade, a fly-past and fireworks. The highlight of the day was the Lighter Owners Association's $16,000 400-foot water dragon that was studded with 7,000 lights and spewed out balls of fire. An official banquet was held at the Victoria Memorial Hall with more than 300 invited guests including the representatives from junior clerical staff and labourers.

The Transcript of the Royal City Day Charter by King George VI of Great Britain reads:

George the Sixth, by the Grace of God, of Great Britain, Ireland and the British Dominions beyond the seas, King, Defender of the Faith; to all to whom these Presents shall come, Greetings.

Whereas the inhabitants of the Town of Singapore in Our Colony of Singapore are a body corporate by the name and style of the Municipal Commissioners of Singapore; and Whereas We, for divers good causes and considerations Us thereunto moving, are graciously pleased to raise the said Town to the rank of a City.

Now, therefore, know ye that We of Our especial grace and favour and mere motion do by this, Our Royal Charter will, ordain, constitute, declare and appoint that Our said Town shall on the twenty-second day of September in the year of Our Lord one thousand nine hundred and fifty-one and forever thereafter be a City, and shall be called and styled THE CITY OF SINGAPORE, instead of the Town of Singapore, and shall thenceforth have all such rank, liberties, privileges and immunities as are incident to a City.

...

In Witness whereof We have caused these Our letters to be made Patent Witness Ourself at Westminster, the twenty-forth day of July in the fifteenth year of Our Reign.

By warrant under the King's Sign Manual, Napier.

Source: National Library Board Infopedia Talk

LOCAL SITCOMS THAT MADE IT OVERSEAS

- **Under One Roof** (Malaysia, Indonesia, Thailand, Australia, USA)
- **Phua Chu Kang** (Malaysia, Indonesia, Brunei)
- **Living with Lydia** (Malaysia, Thailand, Myanmar, Indonesia, Macau, Hong Kong, Australia, USA)

- **Oh Carol!** (Malaysia, Hong Kong)
- **Maggi & Me** (Malaysia, Cambodia, USA)
- **Achar** (Malaysia, USA)

Sources: *Essential Singapore*; *Time Out Singapore*

SECRET SOCIETIES

Nominally descendants of anti-Manchu organisations known as the *tiandihui* (or Heaven and Earth Society), the first Chinese secret societies came with the early immigrants and boasted a membership roll of some 5,000 by the mid-1800s. Their influence in the Chinese community enabled them to mobilise the Chinese for gang violence. In May 1854, a ten-day riot broke out between the Hokkiens and Teochews, leading to five hundred deaths and three hundred homes destroyed. The entire vice industry in Singapore – gambling, opium and prostitution – was very much in their hands as well. To rein them in, the government moved to ban the secret societies in 1890 through the Societies Ordinance. Ten major secret societies were broken up as they refused to register themselves.

NATURE VERSUS NURTURE

I n 1984, the government introduced the Graduate Mothers Priority Scheme - this policy offered incentives to female university graduates. The fear was that graduate women were delaying motherhood or forgoing marriage and children to pursue their careers instead. Graduate women were encouraged to have more children in return for cash incentives. In contrast, the least educated women were encouraged to stop at one or two children, in return for a cash grant of S$10,000 to CPF accounts. This policy sparked a furore among Singaporeans and led to lengthy debates in Parliament on the topic of "nature" versus "nurture". There was considerable public criticism – including from graduate women – over this attempt at social engineering. Not surprisingly, this scheme was quietly dropped because of the political backlash it engendered.

"Equal employment opportunities, yes, but we shouldn't get our women into jobs where they cannot, at the same time, be mothers ... You just can't be doing a full-time heavy job like that of a doctor or engineer and run a home and bring up children."

- Lee Kuan Yew's National Day Rally Speech, *The Straits Times*, 15 August 1983

SENTOSA'S IGNOMINIOUS PAST

S entosa was once known as Pulau Blakang Mati which in Malay means "island of death from behind" in Malay. How did the island acquire such an unpropitious name ? One account attributed it to murder and piracy in the island's past. A second claimed that the island was haunted by warrior spirits buried at Pulau Brani. A third account claims that an outbreak of disease on the island in the late 1840s almost wiped out the original Bugis settlers on the island. A fourth interpretation is that "Dead Back Island" was so-called because of the lack of fertile soil. However, since the island creates a body of still water with no wind, this is perhaps a more plausible explanation from a nautical viewpoint. In a 1972 contest organised by the Singapore Tourist Promotion Board (STPB), the island was renamed Sentosa, a Malay word meaning "peace and tranquillity".

Source: Wikipedia

PRISON ART
· · · · · · ·

A prison sentence needn't mean the end of one's hope or creativity. Between October 1942 and May 1943, Stanley Warren, a British prisoner-of-war during the Japanese Occupation, painted a set of five murals during his internment at Changi. The murals depicted biblical scenes in a European neo-classical style, and they helped to encourage and uplift prisoners' spirits. Warren, who had returned to the UK after the war, made three trips to Singapore to restore the murals when they were rediscovered in 1958. Today, a replica of the murals can be found at the Changi Chapel and Museum on Upper Changi Road North. However, the original artwork remains under restricted access at Changi Air Base.

BEFORE RAFFLES
· · · · · · ·

M odern Singapore was founded in 1819 by Sir Stamford Raffles, but it could all have been so different. In 1703, an English trader named Alexander Hamilton stopped over at Johor on his way from India to China. He called in on an acquaintance, the Abdu'l Jalil Ri'ayat Shah, who had just been crowned Bendahara-Sultan.

Hamilton wrote: "The Sultan treated me very kindly, and made me a present of the island of Sincapure [sic], but I told him it could be of no use to a private person, tho' a proper place for a Company to settle a colony on, lying in the centre of trade, and being accommodated with good rivers and safe harbours, so conveniently situated, that all winds served shipping both to go out and come into those rivers. The soil is black and fat; and the woods abound in good masts for shipping, and timber for building. I have seen large beans growing wild in the woods, not inferior to the best in Europe for taste and beauty; and sugar-cane five or six inches round growing wild also." Hamilton demurred, seeing no use for the island, and so lost the chance to become the founder of Singapore and have roads, schools and a hotel named after him!

Source: *Singapore: A 700-Year History*

KARUNG GUNI
· · · · · · ·

Karung Guni men were traditionally rag-and-bone dealers who went from door to door to buy discarded household articles or old newspapers which they then resold. "Karung" or "karong" means "sack" and the term "karung guni" originated sometime before 1940 to describe travelling hawkers who went around with a sack slung over their shoulders or with sacks in baskets tied to two ends of a pole, balanced across their shoulders. The cry "karung guni", accompanied by a tooting horn, tells you that they are nearby. In recent years, falling scrap prices have put a dent in their earnings. As one person observed, "People use the computer to see the news". This means fewer old newspapers to collect and resell!

LONGEST BUS
· · · · · · ·

Singapore once had Asia's longest bus – 19-metre Volvo B10MA-60 – first introduced in the 1990s. The articulated bus was eventually sold to a New Zealand bus company in 2006 as there were issues with its manoeuvrability as well as the amount of road space it took up. The bus is now used as a school bus in New Zealand.

WHO WOULD YOU RATHER WORK FOR?
· · · · · · ·

The top employers of choices for fresh graduates in Singapore are (in no particular order), DBS Bank, Rolls-Royce, Unilever, Singapore Airlines, Microsoft, Capitaland and the Ministry of Education.

CHINESE FUNERAL RITUALS

The Chinese believe that the most important thing in life is have a good death. Here are a handful of traditional rituals. Not all are still observed. Some have been updated to keep up with the times.

1. Gathering of the family: it is considered unfilial to be absent at one's parent's deathbed.

2. Wearing of funeral garments: there are five grades of funeral garments to denote the relationship of mourners to the deceased. The closer the kinship, the coarser the cloth used. After the funeral, mourners should avoid wearing red, yellow and brown for the mourning period lasting 49 or 100 days, and pieces of cloth matching their mourning garments are pinned on their sleeves during this time.

3. Performing rituals to help the deceased move on into the next world: cleansing and dressing, coffining, burning sacrifices, engaging Buddhist monks or Taoist priests to conduct rites.

4. Holding the funeral wake: the wake lasts for three, five or seven days. Family members are expected to keep all-night vigils.

5. Installing the deceased as an ancestor: placing a picture of the deceased and an urn on the ancestral altar at home or installing an ancestral tablet in a temple.

FROM BITNET TO TECHNET TO THE INTERNET

It is little known that Singapore began building its internet as early as 1991. Dr. Tan Tin Wee, a newly returned biochemist at the National University of Singapore, realised that NUS did not have the sort of computing infrastructure he was used to when studying in Britain. But NUS did offer a rudimentary connection to the outside world – Bitnet. Very soon, Dr. Tan was sending email, FTP, visiting online bulletin boards and databases. This did not go unnoticed. In his own words, "they noticed that I, coming out of the medical school, was one of the biggest users of the internet — and I wasn't downloading porn." In 1991, he was appointed to build NUS's Technet – its gateway to the internet. With this $3.5 million project, Singapore took its first steps into the Internet age with dial-up modems, FTP protocols and Multi-User Dungeons and Dragons (MUDD).

MUST-SEE ATTRACTIONS OF THE 1970S
· ·

- Jurong Bird Park: World's largest, here's our newest attraction no visitor should miss. From arctic dwellers to birds-of-paradise, vultures to flamingos, 50 landscaped acres contain over 7,000 birds of more than 350 species. See some in mock-natural habitats, others flying free in 5-acre netted Falls Aviary where a 100-ft waterfall thunders beneath Rainbow Bridge. Tour on foot or by tram-car. Lakeside restaurant, too. Open daily 10 am–7 pm (no admission after 6). Adult general admission: $1.50; Falls Aviary: $1. Children: half price.

- Japanese Garden, Jurong: A 32-acre typical Japanese garden on a man-made island in Jurong Lake, landscaped into various unique smaller gardens by a Japanese expert. A $3-million project. Open daily 9 am–10 pm. Admission: 40 cents; Children: half price.

- Botanic Gardens, Nassim Rd: Frisky monkeys, swans to feed, gorgeous rare orchids to admire. Stroll amidst avenues of trees, relax by miniature lake and pavilion. Explore virgin jungle area, too. Daily 6 am–10 pm. Free.

- Van Kleef Aquarium, Clemenceau Ave: Sea turtles, fierce moray eels, small sharks are amongst over 300 species of fish and sea life. Brightly coloured tropical and Malaysian fish included. Daily 10 am–8.30 pm. Adults: 30 cents; Children: 20 cents.

- Tiger Balm Gardens (Haw Par Villa), Pasir Panjang Rd: Just for fun, with still life replicas of animals to rival Disneyland. Extravagant statues from Chinese mythology, including lurid depictions of purgatory. A whole hillside of grottos, caves and pavilions must be seen to be believed. Free.

- Tiger Oil House of Jade, No. 3, Nassim Rd: One of the finest collections of jade art objects to be found anywhere. Admission free. Passes obtainable from Haw Par Bros Pte Ltd, 3-B, Lim Teck Kim Rd. Open daily 9 am–6 pm.

- Chinatown, btwn. South Bridge & New Bridge Rds: Old China lives on, teeming with colour and vitality. Hear the crash of gongs, clicking bamboo sticks, vendors' cries, vehement bargaining. See strange merchandise, food stalls, herb shops, temples, colourful funeral processions. By night, brightly lit and busier than ever.

- National Museum, Stamford Rd: Get a fascinating insight into Singapore's past from rare archeological relics, historical exhibits and documents. Look at fine specimens of local flora and fauna and craft displays. Daily 9 am–5.30 pm. Sundays, holidays 10 am–1 pm. Free.

- Art Museum, University of Singapore, Bukit Timah: Enjoy a fine collection of painting and sculpture from here and other nearby countries … also pottery, pewterware, interesting ceramics. Weekdays 9 am–4.30 pm. Saturdays 9 am–1 pm. Closed Sundays.

- Seah Gallery, Tudor Court, Tanglin Rd: Home gallery of famous local batik artist, Seah Kim Joo. Batik paintings, Chinese finger paintings, metal sculptures, wood cut/lino cut prints, reproductions of batik paintings. Daily 10 am–6 pm.

- Mandai Gardens, Mandai Rd: Just picture 10 acres of orchids! A breathtaking vista to thrill anyone who ever thought an orchid spelt tropical romance. See rare Malaysian blooms and exotic new hybrids. Tropical Water Garden, too. Daily 9 am–6 pm. Adults: $1. Children and tour group members: 50 cents.

- Housing Estates (biggest are Queenstown and Toa Payoh): Part of the "New" Singapore. Government-subsidised multi-storey flats solve the housing problem for thousands of middle and lower income Singaporeans.

- Rubber Plantations (Upper Bukit Timah, Tampines Rd, etc.): It's fascinating and fun to see for yourself how trees are tapped and rubber produced. A cool, shady outing. Arrange through Tourist Promotion Board.

- Kelongs (Changi, Punggol Point): To many, they symbolise Singapore. Constructed off-shore of wooden poles, a fishing kelong uses flickering lights to attract and nets to trap the fish. Visit one, and see how it's done. Enquire Tourist Promotion Board.

- Kranji Cemetery and War Memorial, Woodlands Rd: Tranquil and beautiful with view across Straits as far as Johore. A moving tribute to those who died here in the Pacific War.

- MacRitchie and Seletar Reservoirs: Pretty parklands contrast vividly with untamed tropical surroundings. MacRitchie has floating, illuminated fountain. At Seletar, see dams and tower.

- Mt Faber, off Telok Blangah (Pasir Panjang) Rd: Here's a panorama to take your breath away! From one of the highest points in Singapore, get an eagle's eye view of the city, harbour, sea and islands beyond. Incomparable sunsets.

- Changi Village and Beach: Lovely spot to get away from it all. Pack a picnic, go beachcombing. See a carefree "kampong" (Malay village). Sunbathe, and at high tide, swim. Changi Village has picturesque shops and many bargains.

Source: *The Singapore Visitor* (free distribution), Mar 1973

KINGS OF SINGAPORE
· · · · · · ·

Ruler	Reign
Sri Tri Buana, also known as Sang Nila Utama	1299–1347
Regnal name: Paduka Sri Pikrama Wira	1347–1362
Regnal name: Sri Rana Wikerma	1362–1375
Regnal name: Paduka Sri Maharaja Birth name: Damar Raja	1375–1389
Regnal name: Sri Sultan Iskandar Shah Birth name: Raja Iskandar Also known as Parameswara	1389–1391

FANDI
· · · · · · ·

Fans of Singapore football would surely know who Fandi Ahmad is. Fandi, as he is popularly known, was the first Singapore player to play and score in a European title competition. Playing for FC Gronigen against Inter Milan, Fandi scored the second goal in a 2-0 match in October 1983. In 1999, Fandi was named one of FC Gronigen's 25 best players and inducted into their Hall of Fame. Four years later, in the 2003, he was included in the club's best XI for the 20th century.

MOBILE NATION
· · · · · · ·

No, you're not just imagining that every other person on the MRT or bus is talking or playing games/listening to music on their mobile phone. In 2019, there were 8,289,900 mobile subscriptions in Singapore, giving it a mobile penetration rate of 154.1%. Android phones are the devices of choice with the iPhone coming in second.

Sources: *The Straits Times*; Admob

OLD CHINESE AND TAMIL NAMES OF STREETS

T hough the British gave official names to the streets of Singapore, the local people came up with their own. The Malays, while embracing names like "Jalan Sultan", generally referred to places in reference to the nearest kampongs. For example, "Kampong Jawa" for the Arab Street area, and "Kampong Kapur" for the vicinity of Weld Road.

English Name	Local Name (Tamil Names in bold)
Amoy Street	Ma Cho Keng Au – "The back of Ma Cho Temple"
Arab Street	Jiawa Koi – "Javanese street" **Pukadei Sadakku** – "Street of the flower shops"
Beach Road	**Kadal Karei Sadakku** – "Road by the seaside"
Bukit Timah Road	Be Chia Lo Boi – "End of the horse-carriage street"
Clyde Terrace	**Irumpu Pasar** – "Iron market"
Collyer Quay	Tho Kho Au – "At the back of the godowns"
Esplanade	Twa Kok Cheng Chau Po – "The grass field in front of the great court" **January Thidal** – "January place" so named from the sports held on New Year's Day.
Eu Tong Sen Street/ New Bridge Road	Dai Po Yi Ma Lou – "Second road at the big slope"
High Street	Twa Kok Koi – "Supreme Court street"
Hill Street/ Victoria Street	Siu Po Yi Ma Lou – "Second road at the little slope"
Hokkien Street	Cho Be Chia Koi – "The street where horse-carriages are made"
Kampong Java Road	Ang Mo Phun – "European tombs"
Market Street	**Chetty Theruvu** – "Chetties' Street"

Macao Street	Po Li Pi – "The side of the police [ie Central Station]"
Neil Road	Gu Chia Chwi Kia Lo – "The steep street of Kreta Ayer"
North Bridge Road	Siu Po Dai Ma Lou – "Main road at the little slope"
Orchard Road	Tang Leng Pa Sat Koi – "Tanglin market street"
Queen Street	Siu Po Sam Ma Lou – "Third road at the little slope"
South Bridge Road	Dai Po Dai Ma Lou – "Main road at the big slope"
Stamford Road	Lau Chwi Khe – "Flowing water stream"
Sultan Gate	Phah Thi Koi – "The street of the iron smiths"
Tanglin, Upper	Vampumalei – "Whampoa's hill"
Thomson Road	Thanir Pilei Sadakku – "Water pipe street"
Upper Hokkien Street	Lam Pa Koi – "Swamp street"

SINGAPORE'S TALLEST
· · · · · ·

Guoco Tower (formerly Tanjong Pagar Centre), standing at 290 metres, is the tallest building in Singapore. This breaks the record held for more than twenty years by UOB Plaza, One Raffles Place and Republic Plaza, all of which stand at 280m.

GHOST ISLAND
· · · · · ·

Fans of pirate tales will love this. Pulau Hantu, literally meaning "Ghost Island" in Malay, is one of Singapore's offshore islands. Thought to be haunted, legend has it that pirates hid loot on the island. In order to deter unwelcome visitors, they planted flickering lights that gave the illusion of floating spirits. Today, the island is a popular camping ground and boasts one of the cleanest beaches off the main island.

UNIQUE FEATS
• • • • • • •

- The world domino topple record (303,621 dominoes toppled out of 303,628 set up) was set in Singapore on 18 August 2003 by a 24-year-old woman from China.

- At the An-Nur Mosque Family Day on 17 September 2006, 724 people simultaneously pulled their *teh tarik* (literally, pulled tea) before downing the frothy and milky brew.

- 2,402 participants used sign language to sign the words to the song *Uniquely You* simultaneously, making it the greatest number of people signing words, on 9 August 2005 as part of the National Day celebrations at Marina South. The event was organised by the Singapore Association for the Deaf.

- In 1989, Anglo-Chinese School played musical chairs for 3.5 hours, starting with 8,328 participants. The event became the world's biggest game of musical chairs.

- Out of 24 people who participated, Michael Chia, Fadzli Hussen and Norman Oman broke the world record by sitting through 36 films running for 72 hours outside Plaza Singapura from 22 to 25 July 2004. Contestants were allowed 5-minute rest breaks between each movie and a 15-minute break for every third film.

- At the Cram Jam organised by SMRT on 11 February 2007 at the Bishan Depot, 526 people from the Home Team Academy managed to pack themselves into one train carriage.

- On 22 July 2006, 150 chefs from the Society of Professional Chefs (Singapore) and Society of Chinese Cuisine Chefs took over an hour to build the tallest ice kachang ever recorded. Towering 3 metres over Smith Street, the ice dessert used 3,800 kilogrammes of ice, 68 litres of sugar syrup and 30 kg of ingredients. It was part of the Singapore Food Festival, in conjunction with the Chinatown Business Association.

Source: Singapore Book of Records

A SYMBOL OF PEACE FROM CHINA

Singapore currently hosts two giant pandas from the China Wildlife Conservation Association. This was announced following a meeting between President Hu Jintao and President S R Nathan in 2009. The loan of the two pandas represents the close relationship between Singapore and China as the Republic celebrated the 20th anniversary of Sino-Singapore relations.

China has only extended this unique privilege to fewer than 10 countries, including the United States, Japan, Thailand, Austria, Australia and Spain.

SINGAPORE RAILWAY STATION

Also known as Keppel Road Railway Station or Singapore Railway Station, Tanjong Pagar Railway Station was a railway terminus providing train services between Singapore and Thailand until July 2011. Opened in 1932, the station's facade features four reliefs in white marble, symbolising Agriculture, Industry, Commerce and Transport, which were sculpted by Rudolfo Nolli. In the station hall, the wall panels depict Malayan scenes such as rice planting, rubber tapping and tin mining. After Singapore's independence in 1965 the status of the railway station was contested. A "Welcome to Malaysia" sign once hung above the station entrance to assert Malaysian ownership. This was removed in 2004. On 1 July 2011, railway operations, together with customs, immigration and quarantine facilities, were relocated to Woodlands Train Checkpoint (WTCP) on 1 July 2011. The old station building at Tanjong Pagar was gazetted as a national monument on 9 April 2011.

HOW TO SPOT A FAKE SINGAPORE BANK NOTE
· · · · · · ·

Singapore's currency notes have extensive security features that make counterfeiting extremely difficult. So here's what to look out for to tell real from fake:

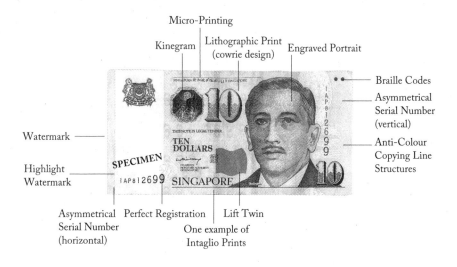

Micro-Printing

Kinegram Lithographic Print (cowrie design) Engraved Portrait

Braille Codes

Asymmetrical Serial Number (vertical)

Watermark

Anti-Colour Copying Line Structures

Highlight Watermark

Asymmetrical Serial Number (horizontal) Perfect Registration Lift Twin

One example of Intaglio Prints

Anti-Colour Copying Line Structures

Watermark

Highlight Watermark

Security Thread Perfect Registration

Source: "Know Your Money", Monetary Authority of Singapore

A SELECTION OF LEE KUAN YEW QUOTES

. . . .

"Repression, Sir, is a habit that grows. I am told it is like making love, it is always easier the second time! The first time there may be pangs of conscience, a sense of guilt. But once embarked on this course with constant repetition you get more and more brazen in the attack." (1956)

"Please remember we do not pretend to be virtuous. Hypocrisy is not a feature of Singapore's leadership." (1971)

"If you don't include your women graduates in your breeding pool and leave them on the shelf, you would end up a more stupid society ... So what happens? There will be less bright people to support dumb people in the next generation. That's a problem." (1983)

"Now if democracy will not work for the Russians, a white Christian people, can we assume that it will naturally work with Asians?" (1991)

"If you are a troublemaker ... it's our job to politically destroy you ... Everybody knows that in my bag I have a hatchet, and a very sharp one. You take me on, I take my hatchet, we meet in the cul-de-sac." (1997)

"The Bell curve is a fact of life. The blacks on average score 85 per cent on IQ and it is accurate, nothing to do with culture. The whites score on average 100. Asians score more ..." (1997)

"If I tell Singaporeans – we are all equal regardless of race, language, religion, culture. Then they will say, 'Look, I'm doing poorly. You are responsible.' But I can show that from British times, certain groups have always done poorly, in Mathematics and in Science. But I'm not God, I can't change you. But I can encourage you, give you extra help to make you do, say maybe, 20 per cent better." (2002)

REVENGE IS A DISH BEST SERVED SPICY

In December 1984, caretaker Ayakanno Marimuthu was reported missing by his wife when he did not return home from a trip to Malaysia. Three years later, in January 1987, the police were informed that three Indian men had murdered the hot-tempered and physically abusive Marimuthu. They had chopped up his body into pieces and made a curry out of it. The curry was placed in garbage bags and dumped in roadside rubbish bins. The murder allegedly took place in the caretaker's quarters of Orchard Road Presbyterian Church on Penang Road. However, no body parts or weapons were found and due to insufficient evidence, no one was convicted.

Source: *Singapore the Encyclopedia*

ORIGINS OF HOKKIEN MEE

It is believed that Hokkien migrant workers from the Fujian province of China, who toiled in the local noodle (mee) factories, invented this dish in Singapore. They would gather around Rochor Road at the end of the day with bags of extra noodles from the factory and fry them at night. Within a short period of time, copycat hawkers had set up stalls in the vicinity. Many older Singaporeans still call this dish "Rochor mee". Hokkien mee is made by pan-frying a mix of yellow wheat noodles and rice vermicelli. It is flavoured with prawn stock and topped with prawns, squid rings and thin slices of pork. The ingredients used for the soup stock are often a trade secret but might include a mix of pig's bones, clams, dried and fried flat fish, sugar cane and prawns. The trick is to steep the noodles in stock and fry them until they absorb the flavours of the stock.

Source: *Singapore the Encyclopedia*

BUNGALOW OR MANSION

The term "bungalow" in British English refers to a small one-storey house. In Singapore, however, bungalows are large, usually two-storeyed, mansions.

SITTING PRETTY

O ne of the most renowned plastic surgeons in Asia and the surgeon of choice for many celebrities and notables, Singaporean doctor Woffles Wu, pioneered an innovative non-surgical facelift that involves minimal pain, leaves no scars and allows patients to resume activities within a few days of the operation. Many consider this procedure, called the Woffles Lift, to be the most important advancement in facelift surgery, and Wu is the only Asian to be featured in the book *Aesthetic Surgery* (2005), which reveals the world's top cosmetic surgeons. Speaking of books, Wu's mother affectionately named him Woffles after a rabbit from Enid Blyton's book, *The Magic Faraway Tree*.

WE, THE CITIZENS OF SINGAPORE

T he Singapore Citizenship Ordinance (1957) granted Singapore citizenship to all residents who were born in Singapore or the Federation of Malaya, British citizens who had been resident for two years and others who had been resident for ten years. Upon Singpore's merger with Malaysia on 16 September 1963, all Singapore citizens became Malaysian citizens, while retaining their Singapore citizenship. When Singapore gained independence on 9 August 1965, all Singaporeans who were Singapore citizens as of 16 September 1963 were recognised as such, with no change in their status. Citizenship was eventually incorporated into the Constitution of the Republic of Singapore.

THE QUEST FOR STARDOM

T he Quests, an all-male quartet, were arguably the most successful local band of the 1960s. Having started out by performing covers of British and American songs, they went on to record a number of original tracks. Their signature tune, "Shanty" became the first song by a local band to reach the top of the Singapore charts, displacing "I Should Have Known Better" by The Beatles, and staying at Number 1 for 12 weeks.

IDENTIFYING THE SINGAPORE GIRLS
· · · · · · ·

In 1972 Pierre Balmain, a French haute couture designer, was hired by Singapore Airlines (SIA) to redesign the traditional Malay *sarong kebaya* for its stewardesses. He added distinctive borders around the hem, neck and cuffs of the *kebaya*. Since then, the uniform has gained worldwide recognition as part of SIA's signature branding. There are four *kebaya* colours that represent the ranking of the Singapore Girls:

Blue uniform: Flight stewardess

Green uniform: Leading stewardess

Red uniform: Chief stewardess

Plum uniform: In-flight manager

BABY MAKING
· · · · · · ·

In 1991, the government began offering cash bonuses to couples to entice them to have more children. And, quite astonishingly, the local newspaper published tips on the more physical aspects of procreating, such as making love in the back seat of a car. They even included directions to some of the "darkest, most secluded and most romantic spots". Very helpfully, they suggested covering the car windows with newspapers for more privacy.

Sources: *New York Times*, 29 Apr 2008; Channel NewsAsia, 22 Jun 2010

BRAS BASAH ROAD
· · · · · · ·

Bras Basah Road derives its name from the practice of drying wet rice on the banks of the Stamford Canal in colonial Singapore. In G.D. Coleman's 1836 Map of Singapore, Bras Basah was spelt "Beras Basah". "Beras" means rice with the husks removed and "basah" means "wet" in Malay. In the earlier Jackson's Plan of 1822, this road was known by two names – Church Street for the section running from Beach Road to North Bridge Road, and Selegy Street for the section running from North Bridge Road to Selegie Hill.

WHAT SINGAPOREANS DO WHEN THEY ARE ONLINE

In 2017, 86.6% of Singapore households had access to the internet. On the average, Singaporeans spend 12 hours and 42 minutes on digital devices, out of which 3 hours and 12 minutes were spent on mobile phones. In a study by consultancy Ernst & Young, 1,000 people aged 18 to 69 were polled and revealed the following.

Top online activities people engaged in at least once a day

Reading personal emails......................... 90% (of respondents)
Online messaging and calling 79%
Social media and networks.. 71%
Work and business purposes 57%
News & sports updates 53%
Games.. 29%

Source: comScore, Inc. (Press releases in Mar 2009, Apr 2010)

SINGAPORE RIVER

The operation was massive;
designed to give new life
to the old lady.
We have cleaned out
Her arteries, removed
detritus and slit,
created a by-pass
for the old blood.
Now you can hardly tell
her history.

We have become
so health-conscious
the heart
can sometimes be troublesome.

– Lee Tzu Pheng, Singapore Poet

HIGHS AND LOWS
. . . .

R ecord keeping for local weather began in 1929. The lowest temperature ever recorded in Singapore (since records began in 1929) is 19.4°C (66.9°F) on 31 January 1934. The highest is 36°C (96.8°F) which was recorded on 26 March 1998. With climate change, the decade 2010 to 2019 was the warmest ever, with a mean daily temperature of 27.94°C.

Source: National Environment Agency

MALAY ICON: P. RAMLEE
. . . .

P. Ramlee is often considered the icon of Malay entertainment in Singapore, Malaysia and Sumatra for his contributions to the movie and music industry during his career. Born Teuku Zakaria bin Teuku Nyak Puteh, he was discovered in 1948 by B.S. Rajhans. Rajhans is often regarded as the founding father of Malay cinema. P. Ramlee's crowning moment was when he won the Best Actor Award at the 1957 Asian Film Festival in Tokyo, for his dual roles in *Anak-ku Sazali* (My Son Sazali). In 1964 P. Ramlee left Singapore for Kuala Lumpur, to join Merdeka Film Productions. In his twenty five year career, he acted in 65 movies and directed 34 feature films, 16 of which were shot in Singapore. He also composed the music and wrote the lyrics for more than 250 songs.

GET YOUR ICE CREAM HERE
. . . .

T raditional ice-cream hawkers have been a local delight in Singapore for years. They offer a huge variety of ice-cream flavours, from the chocolate and vanilla to sweetcorn, red bean or yam. Customers can choose whether they want their block of ice cream in a slice of pink and green pandan-flavoured bread (particularly popular as the bread soaks up the melting ice cream)or as a sandwich between two wafer biscuits. If you ask for a "mix", the vendor scoops a random variety of different flavours into a plastic cup for you to enjoy. This sweet treat now retails for S$1.20.

WALLS THAT SPEAK

"The turned up roofs, the squeezed tenement houses, the leprous walls of Chinatown; so much decrepitude condemned as unfit, yet which must go on lodging many thousands ... Its walls sticky with the slime of years, its day-long banners of family washing thrusting out of every window, and its narrow, crumbling tenements which have a queer habit of falling down of their own accord, in a soft cushion of smothered dust and cries."

Source: *See Singapore*

ULTRA-MARATHON

An ultra-marathon is any sporting event involving running longer than the traditional marathon distance of 42.2 kilometres. In the last edition held in October 2019, the Singapore Ultramarathon covered a distance of 100 kilometres. The run began at Gardens by the Bay East, went down East Coast Park and Tanah Merah Coast Road before looping back at Marina Country Club to end at the start point. Alex Ang took the Men's Solo with a time of 11 hours 37 minutes while Natalie Dau took the Women's Solo in 11 hours 27 minutes and 51 seconds.

Source: AsiaOne, 29 Mar 2010

PLEASE SPEAK "FREELY"

Established at Hong Lim Park on 1 September 2000, Speakers' Corner was intended to provide a place for Singaporeans to express themselves in various ways, such as delivering public speeches, holding peaceful demonstrations, exhibitions or performances. The use of this space is governed by the Public Order (Unrestricted Area) Order 2016. A police permit is required if foreigners are involved in organising and/or participating in an event. In addition, should the event fall under the Public Entertainments and Meetings Act, a separate permit would be required.

BATMAN IN SINGAPORE?

O ne of the most unusual names recorded in Singapore is Batman bin Suparman, the name of a young male, born in 1990 in Singapore to Javanese parents. While the surname Suparman (pronounced Su-par-mun) is quite common among the Javanese, Batman is almost certainly a conscious attempt by his parents at humour.

POPULATION PROFILE

	1970	1990	2010	2019
Total	2,074,500	3,047,100	5,076,700	5,703,600
Residents	2,013,600	2,735,900	3,771,700	4,026,200
Citizens	1,874,800	2,623,700	3,230,700	3,500,900
Permanent Residents	138,800	112,100	541,000	525,300
Non-residents	60,900	311,200	1,305,000	1,677,400

Source: Singapore Department of Statistics

PUBLIC HOUSING PARADISE

O ver 83 per cent of Singaporeans live in public housing, and desirable units have gone for several hundreds of thousands of dollars, even a million dollars, on the resale market. In August 2019, a 39th floor unit at City View@Boon Keng was sold for a record S$1,205,000. This unit was touted to be in a prime city fringe location that straddled two Mass Rapid Transit (MRT) lines.

LOITERING AND CONGREGATION LAW

In Singapore, the police have the right to stop and question you anytime. You are required, by law, to provide information to a police officer if and when asked. You must be able to explain your presence in any location. If the police suspect that you, and a group of five or more, are gathering with the intention to commit a crime, you could be taken in and it is considered an unlawful assembly.

Source: Attorney-General's Chambers

ANIMALS AT THE SINGAPORE ZOO

Number of species: **300**; 24 per cent of which are threatened
Number of specimens: **2,400**
Area: **26** hectares
Number of visitors annually: **190,000**

THE KING OF KATONG

Chew Joo Chiat, well-known Chinese land and coconut plantation owner, bought such a large swathe of land in the east of Singapore that he was dubbed "King of Katong". On this land, which encompassed his vast coconut estate, he built a road network. Unsurprisingly, he named them all after himself - Joo Chiat Road, Joo Chiat Place, Joo Chiat Lane and Joo Chiat Terrace. Though he built and maintained the roads at his own expense, he later donated them to the government. That area is now the famous Joo Chiat neighbourhood, popular for its good food as well as its colourful nightlife. Today, much of the architectural heritage has remained unchanged as many of the pre-war shophouses and homes that line Joo Chiat Road have been gazetted for conservation.

Source: *Toponymics: A Study of Singapore Street Names*

CULTURAL MEDALLION AWARDS

The Cultural Medallion is Singapore's pinnacle award for the arts. It is conferred on individuals with outstanding achievements in dance, theatre, literature, music, photography, art and film. Instituted in March 1979 by Minister for Culture, Ong Teng Cheong, it is administered by the National Arts Council. Past winners include playwright Kuo Pao Kun, musician Jeremy Monteiro, artist Tan Swie Hian and ceramist Iskandar Jalil.

PRIVATE TUTOR WANTED

Due to stiff competition and an obsession over good academic results in Singapore, the country's private tuition market has become serious business. It was estimated to be worth S$1.4 billion in 2018, with seven in ten parents sending their children (including young pre-schoolers) for lessons in one of the 950 tuition or 'enrichment' centres.

LEFT AT THE DOOR

CHIJMES, the entertainment and dining complex located at Victoria Street, was a Catholic convent, school and orphanage - the Convent of the Holy Infant Jesus (CHIJ). In 1942, it was reported that an average of 50 unwanted babies were left at the orphanage's side gate every month. This became known as the "Baby Gate" or the "Gate of Hope".

SMS NATION

According to the Singapore Department of Statistics, the total number of SMS text messages sent and received in Singapore in 2009 was 23,286,009. It has since dwindled to 7,179,100 in 2017 due to the advent of instant messaging apps.

BONDED FOR LIFE

Under the Maintenance of Parents Act, which came into effect in 1995, parents in Singapore above the age of 60 who are unable to support themselves have the right to claim maintenance from their children. Any person disregarding or disobeying an order from the tribunal may be fined up to S$5,000 and/or jailed for up to six months. In the first three years after the Act came into force, more than 400 elderly Singaporeans sought help from the tribunal.

BULLOCK CART WATER

Singapore's Chinese name for its Chinatown is not a direct translation of its English name. The district is known as "Niu Che Shui" (literally "bullock cart water), having derived its name from the bullock-pulled carts that supplied Chinatown with water during the 19th century. Its Malay name, Kreta Ayer, has the same meaning.

THE OLDEST THEATRE

Built in 1929, the Capitol Theatre was a venue for rambunctious cabaret performances until the Shaw brothers turned it into their flagship cinema in 1946. Besides catering to cinemagoers, the building also housed the Capitol Restaurant. Located in the Blue Room, this was a beautiful function room with a high ceiling and a zodiac mosaic that decorated its domed interior.

SHATTERED DREAM

"I was hoping to make Singapore the New York of Malaysia ... my dream is shattered and so we come now to the parting of the ways."

– Malaysian Prime Minister Tunku Abdul Rahman speaking on the separation of Singapore from Malaysia on 9 August 1965.

NEWSWORTHY?
. . . .

The first newspaper to be published in Singapore, *The Singapore Chronicle*, started on 1 January 1824 as a single-sheet, two-page fortnightly, which grew to four pages by 1831. It was discontinued in 1837 in the face of competition from the *Singapore Free Press*, which was launched on 8 October 1935.

TAXIS IN SINGAPORE - NOT SO WELL-LOVED ANYMORE
. . . .

The arrival of ride-hailing apps Grab and Uber in 2013 signalled a marked cooling off in demand for the hitherto well-loved Singapore taxi. The number of taxis in Singapore fell to 23,140 from its peak of 28,736 in 2014. Comfort Delgro, the biggest player with its fleet of iconic blue taxis, saw its fleet shrink to below 10,000, a figure not seen since 2005. With 46,903 private hire vehicles on the roads, the dust in this shakeup of the taxi industry has not settled yet.

ARE YOU ON TIME?
. . . .

Geographically, Singapore should only be 6 hours, 55 minutes and 25 seconds ahead of Greenwich Mean Time (GMT). However, the country runs on Singapore Standard Time which is GMT+8.

IT'S RAINING FISH
. . . .

In February 1861, folks in many areas of Singapore reported a rain of fish following an earthquake. "Fish covered about 50 acres of land as they came down with torrential rains."

Sources: Famous Supernatural Mysteries; *Popular Science*, Jul 1932, Vol 121, No 1.

THE DOOR GODS OF ORCHARD ROAD

The two larger-than-life statues - "door gods" - outside the Hilton Hotel on Orchard Road are in fact modelled after historical figures from the Tang dynasty. One is Wei Chi Jing De, right-hand man of Emperor Tang Tai Zong. The other is Qin Shu Bao, the emperor's trusted swordsman. In one folk tale, they protected the emperor from the Dragon King, who was haunting him night after night. The relentless nightmares stopped only after the two "door gods" were posted at the palace gates. As they could not be deployed around the clock, the emperor had portraits of them pasted on the palace gates instead. The tradition of placing "door gods" to keep away wandering ghosts and spirits was born.

Fabricated in 1975, the statues are 2.7 metres tall and weigh three tonnes each. It took eight people nearly half a year to mould them, and a special kiln with larger doors had to be built to fire them.

ICE CREAM!

The first ice cream in Singapore was manufactured by the Singapore Cold Storage Company in 1923. Set up in 1903, the company is the oldest established supermarket operator in Singapore. The first Cold Storage store opened in the 1930s on Orchard Road.

Sources: Cold Storage; *A History of Modern Singapore 1819–2005*

PHOTO OF BRAD PITT, ANYONE?

Hollywood films have always been extremely popular in Singapore. Even in the 1930s, they accounted for 70 per cent of all films shown in the cinemas. The rest were British, Chinese, Malay and Indian films. In the 1950s and 1960s, film star photos were distributed as freebies to boost the sales of entertainment publications and food products.

MRT TRIVIA
· · · · · · ·

- There are currently 122 stations in operation (as of 2019).
- The deepest station is Bencoolen on the Downtown Line at 43 metres below ground.
- The largest station is Dhoby Ghaut - the North-South, North East and Circle Lines converge here.
- Toa Payoh was the first MRT station to be completed on 5 August 1985.
- The 20-kilometre long North East Line (NEL) is one of the most high-tech tunnels in the world – it was the first fully-underground, automated and driverless rapid transit line.

THEEMITHI (FIRE-WALKING)
· · · · · · ·

Theemithi (also *Thimithi*) or "fire-walking" is done as part of a religious vow in which a devotee walks on fire in exchange for a wish or blessing granted by the Goddess Draupadi. *Theemithi* is part of a larger ceremony stretching over a two-and-a-half month period where parts of the *Mahabharata* (one of the two major Sanskrit epics of ancient India) is re-enacted, totalling up to 18 distinguishable rites.

Fire-walking is an international Hindu ceremony which originated in South India. It is practised not only in India and Singapore but even in countries such as South Africa – wherever there is a South Asian population.

The Goddess Draupadi is the heroine of the *Mahabharata* and is a common village goddess, or *amman* ("mother" goddess). She presides over the fire-walking ceremony in South Indian rituals, just like Mariamman, the principal goddess of Sri Mariamman Temple, and this could be one of the reasons why this temple is the location for the fire-walking ceremony in Singapore. Sri Mariamman Temple also happens to be the oldest and largest Hindu temple in Singapore and *theemithi* has been practised here since 1840.

In 1997, an estimated 2,500 people turned up for the fire-walking ritual with up to 10 per cent of them being Chinese. More than 20,000 turned up for the penance rituals, starting several weeks before the fire-walking.

LANGUAGES SPOKEN AT HOME
· · · · · ·

Language	1990 (%)	2000 (%)	2010 (%)	2015 (%)
English	18.8	23.0	32.3	36.9
Mandarin	23.7	35.0	35.6	34.9
Chinese Dialects (non-Mandarin)	39.6	23.8	14.3	12.2
Malay	14.3	14.1	12.2	10.7
Tamil	2.9	3.2	2.3	3.3

Source: Singapore Department of Statistics

PHILATELY
· · · · · ·

Singapore Post produces more than a million pieces of stamps annually. Each stamp design can take up to two years from conception to production. Some notable past designs include profiles of British monarchs, HDB blocks (1963), the Sentosa Satellite Dish (1971), a series of four stamps depicting people with disabilities for the International Year of Disabled Persons (1981) and a series dedicated to children's toys with pictures of plastic figurines, toy cars and a blonde-haired, blue-eyed doll (2002).

Sources: SingPost; CS Philatelic Agency

UNLUCKY STRIKE
· · · · · ·

Records on lightning fatalities in Singapore show an average of 0.35 deaths per million population (in 2000–2003), as compared to 0.6 in the United States, 0.2 in the United Kingdom and 1.5 in South Africa.

Source: National Environment Agency

HEARTLANDERS
. . . .

'Heartlanders' is a term coined by former Prime Minister Goh Chok Tong and popularised by the media. Goh first used this term in a National Day speech in 1999, juxtaposing "heartlanders" with "cosmopolitans". He described the latter as being international in outlook; English-speaking; employed in high-skilled and high-income sectors, highly mobile and able to adapt to living or working overseas. Heartlanders, on the other hand, were more likely to speak Singlish; live in public housing estates; be employed locally; and be less mobile than cosmopolitans (not by choice) and are generally more parochial (implied).

Source: *Singapore the Encyclopedia*

A BARRAGE LIKE NO OTHER
. . . .

The Marina Barrage, a dam built across the 350-metre wide Marina Channel, created Singapore's 15th reservoir. Together with the Punggol and Serangoon reservoirs, the Marina Reservoir supplies more than 10 per cent of Singapore's water demand. Located in the Central Business District, it is the Republic's largest catchment measuring 10,000 hectares. Besides being a source of water, the Marina Barrage is also part of a comprehensive flood control scheme. It has become a well-loved recreational spot for picnics, kite flying and shooting the breeze.

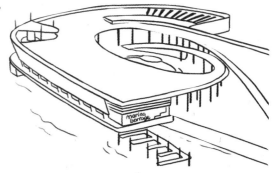

Source: Public Utilities Board

MERLIONS
· · · · · · ·

How many Merlions are there in Singapore, officially recognised by the Singapore Tourism Board? Four.

- The original statue at Merlion Park, Marina Bay.
- The two-metre tall cub statue standing behind the original statue.
- The three-metre tall glazed polymarble statue at Tourism Court (near Grange Road), completed in 1995.
- The three-metre tall polymarble statue placed on Mount Faber's Faber Point.

In addition, variations on the Merlion statue can be found at the Merlion Restaurant in Cupertino in California, USA, and in Nambo Paradise Botanical Gardens in Tateyama, Chiba, Japan. In London there is a Merlion proudly watching over the Mystic East area of Chessington World of Adventures and there are a couple of replica statues in China, too.

MIRACULOUSLY STRONG
· · · · · · ·

The Church of Our Lady of Lourdes on Ophir Road was bombed by the Japanese during World War II. However, while nearby buildings on the church grounds were severely damaged, the church itself remained, incredibly, unscathed. Divine intervention, perhaps?

INTIMATE OPERATION
· · · · · · ·

The first successful sex change surgery in Singapore was performed on a man in 1971.

MOMMY, I CAN'T SEE CLEARLY
· · · · · · ·

Singapore has one of the highest rates of myopia in the world. Roughly one in two children under 12 in Singapore wear glasses.

FILM CLASSIFICATION IN SINGAPORE
· · · · · · ·

(G)	**GENERAL**	Entertainment that is suitable for the whole family.
(PG)	**PARENTAL GUIDANCE**	Suitable for all ages. Parents should guide their young as some scenes may be disturbing to children.
PG 13	**PARENTAL GUIDANCE 13**	Suitable for persons aged 13 and above but parental guidance is advised for children below 13.
NC16	**NO CHILDREN UNDER 16**	Not appropriate for those below 16 years of age, as the film may contain more explicit scenes.
M18	**MATURE 18**	For viewers aged 18 and above, these films may contain mature themes which are more suitable for young adults.
R21	**RESTRICTED 21**	For viewers aged 21 and above, these films may contain adult themes and more explicit scenes. This was known as the R(A) (Restricted Artistic) rating before 2004.

Source: Media Development Authority

PUBLIC HOLIDAYS IN SINGAPORE
. . . . . .

New Year's Day	1 January
Chinese New Year	1st and 2nd day of the Chinese lunar calendar
Good Friday	Friday preceeding Easter Sunday (1st Sunday after the first full moon after the Vernal Equinox)
Labour Day	1 May
Vesak Day (marks the birth, enlightenment and passing on of Buddha)	First full moon in May (common years) or June (leap years)
National Day	9 August
Hari Raya Puasa (marks the end of Ramadan or fasting month)	1st day of the tenth month of the Islamic calendar
Deepavali (Festival of Lights)	Begins late Ashwin, seventh month of the luni-solar Hindu calendar
Hari Raya Haji (day of pilgrimage)	10th day of the twelfth month of the Islamic calendar
Christmas Day	25 December

BUILDING THE ISTANA
. . . .

Built in 1869, the Istana is the official residence and office of the President of Singapore. The 106-acre estate was once part of a nutmeg plantation and the building was officially known as Government House before Singapore attained full self-government in 1959.

The entire brickwork, exterior plastering and most of the flooring and interior work were completed by Indian convict labour. They were paid 20 cents a day for their efforts – a lot more than the local coolies, who earned around three to seven cents a day.

ARMENIANS IN SINGAPORE

The Armenians are one of the smallest minority communities in Singapore. Despite their small numbers, they have left an outsized imprint on Singapore in architecture, botany, business and the press. They first came in the 1820s and by the 1830s, these Armenian merchants had begun investing in real estate. In March 1836, the Church of Saint Gregory the Illuminator was consecrated, making it the first church in Singapore. By the 1880s, the Armenians numbered some 100 families.

Armenian notables include Catchick Moses (Movessian) (1812–1892), a co-founder of *The Straits Times*; the Sarkies brothers, founders of the Raffles Hotel; and Agnes Joaquim, after whom the national flower, the *Vanda* Miss Joaquim is named.

Apart from landmarks such as the Church of St Gregory the Illuminator, several streets are named after the Armenians, including Armenian Street, Galiston Avenue, Sarkies Road and St Martin's Drive. Other streets associated with them but have since been expurgated due to development include Armenian Lane off Armenian Street and Narcis Road.

Armenian businesses were badly hit by the Great Depression and then by the Japanese Occupation, with many Armenians being interned. By the 1950s, much of the Armenian community had migrated to Australia or blended peacefully into the larger local communities.

Source: National Library Board Infopedia Talk

SINGAPORE DOLLAR BILLS

On 12 June 1967, Singapore issued its first currency notes as an independent country. They were known as the Orchid series, and they came in denominations of $1, $5, $10, $50, $100 and $1,000. The $25 and $500 notes were introduced in 1972, followed by $10,000 in 1973 – the world's most valuable note, though rarely used.

Between 1976 and 1980, the Bird series was introduced, including a $20 note in 1979.

The Ship series was introduced between 1985 and 1989 in the same denominations but without a $20 note. $2 notes were introduced in 1990.

The current Portrait series was introduced in 1999. The $1 note has been replaced by a $1 coin.

THE FIRST SKYSCRAPER
• • • • • • •

Believe it or not, the Cathay Building at 2 Handy Road was Singapore's first skyscraper at 16 storeys and a height of 83.5 metres. Opened in 1939, it housed a cinema, luxury apartments, a fancy restaurant and a hotel. It was also the island's first air-conditioned cinema and public building.

During the Japanese Occupation, the building was renamed Dai Toa Gekijo (Greater East Asian Theatre) and housed the Japanese Military Information Bureau. After the war, it served briefly as Lord Louis Mountbatten's headquarters before being handed back to its pre-war owners in November 1946.

The main structure has been demolished to develop what is now known as The Cathay, but the facade however has been gazetted as a national monument.

EXTRAVAGANT ART DECO
• • • • • • •

Built at a cost of S$88 million, Parkview Square in Bugis was one of the most expensive and lavish office buildings in Singapore at the time of its construction in 1999. Inspired by the Chanin Building in New York City, it was designed in Art Deco style. Its open plaza features sculptures and statues of famous figures in history such as Abraham Lincoln, Salvador Dalí, Mozart, Isaac Newton, Shakespeare, Plato, Winston Churchill and Albert Einstein. A lobby with a 15 metre high ceiling detailed with handcrafted features adds to the opulence exuded by the building.

MACHINE WASH ONLY
• • • • • • •

The percentage of Singaporeans who owned a washing machine in 1973 was 1.8. By 2003, thirty years later, the percentage had jumped to 92.9.

MILES APART
· · · · · · ·

Here is a sample of the First and Economy class menus on a typical Singapore Airlines flight from London to Singapore. As you can see, you get what you pay for:

SQ 319 London–Singapore

Dinner in First Class	Dinner in Economy Class
Canapes Satay with onion, cucumber and spicy peanut sauce	
Appetisers Chilled malossol caviar with melba toast and condiments OR Spanish iberico air-dried ham garnished with fresh fig, mixed salad	**Appetiser** Marinated prawns with pasta and vegetable salad
Soups Cream of globe artichoke OR Oriental chicken soup with quail egg and mixed vegetables	
Salad Baby lettuce with shaved fennel, dried cranberries and roasted marinated beetroot WITH Sherry vinegar and walnut oil dressing OR Yoghurt citrus dressing	

Main Courses

* Roasted lobster with saffron in chervil and caper butter, sautéed spinach, steamed potato OR
Cantonese-style roasted duck served with selected vegetables and fried noodles OR
Grilled beef fillet served with creamy morel sauce, selected vegetables and mashed potato OR
Roganjosh-style lamb curry with saffron, spiced stuffed capsicums, spinach dumplings and fragrant cumin scented rice OR
** Saffron tagliatelle with creamy assorted mushroom ragout, arugula lettuce and shaved parmesan cheese

Dessert

Opera cake served with vanilla ice cream and espresso coffee sauce

Cheeses

Somerset brie, butlers' secret mature cheddar, wensleydale with cranberries and shropshire blue with quince paste, grapes, nuts and crackers

Fruits

Fresh fruits in season

Main Courses

Stir-fried pork with ginger and spring onion, served with seasonal vegetables and steamed rice OR
Indian tandoori chicken, served with mixed vegetable curry and pilau rice with almonds

Dessert

Häagen-Dazs ice cream

Snack

Cheese and crackers

Hot Beverages

Coffee or Tea

Finalé
A selection of gourmet coffees and fine
teas served with pralines
* Exclusively created by Gordon Ramsay,
London
** Specially prepared meatless selection

SIGN-LANGUAGE WEDDING VOWS
. . . .

On 1 December 1963 three hearing-impaired brothers married three hearing impaired sisters after a year-long courtship in Singapore. They were Leong Teck Heng and Seet Guat Lui, Teck See and Hock Neo, and Teck Choy and Been Neo. Apart from 17-year-old Been Neo, they were all in their twenties, and the couples had paired off according to their ages – eldest brother with eldest sister, middle brother with middle sister and the youngest brother with youngest sister.

MAID TO ORDER
. . . .

One of the world's top employers of foreign domestic workers, Singapore has around 255,800 migrant women employed in this capacity as of 2019. Most of these workers come from the Philippines and Indonesia, while a minority comes from Thailand, Burma (Myanmar), Sri Lanka and India. Approximately one foreign domestic worker is employed in every five households.

Source: Singapore Institute of International Affairs

CHILLI CRAB
· · · · · · ·

C hilli crab is a seafood dish originating from Singapore. It was created in 1950 by Singapore chef, Cher Yam Tian and her husband, Lim Choon Ngee. Mud crabs are commonly used, but other varieties of crab – such as flower crabs or blue swimmer crabs – are used as well. Despite its name, chilli crab is not a particularly spicy dish. Its signature chilli-based sauce is thickened with corn flour and flavoured with garlic, rice vinegar and soy sauce. Beaten egg is used to finish the sauce. It is then garnished with coriander leaves.

The well-loved crustacean delight is commonly **served with bread, steamed or fried *mantou* (Chinese buns), French loaves or toasted bread**, which are used to mop up the sauce. It also goes well with plain white rice.

Before frying, the **crab** is chopped into large pieces and steamed with slices of ginger to remove fishy smells. The crab shell is usually partially cracked before cooking for ease of eating. It is then stir-fried in chilli sauce and other condiments.

HOW TO CHOOSE DURIAN

1. Whole Fruit

2. Pick the durian up (be careful!) and give it a gentle shake. If there is no sound, the fruit is too ripe and it may be bitter and pungent. If there is a sharp knocking sound, the fruit is not ripe enough. What you should be hearing is a dull, subtle knocking sound.

3. The durian should be slightly fragrant. It should not smell too strong, which is an indication of an overly ripe fruit.

Pre-packed

1. Glide your fingers very lightly over the surface of the flesh (over the plastic wrap of course, or you will anger the durian seller). It should feel tender and soft.

2. Smell test as above.

BREAKING EUROPE

Although Singapore is the home of many musicians who have been successful abroad, The Swallows is the only Singaporean band to have had a hit in Europe. "La Obe", released in the 1960s, was a hit in both Singapore and West Germany. It stayed on a radio station's Top 10 chart for three weeks.

927 WINDOWS?

The Old Hill Street Police Station was the largest government building in Singapore when it opened in 1934. Built at a cost of S$634,263, it was a police station and also home to the policemen. Its facade of 927 colourful windows makes this national monument a prominent landmark.

SIMPLE RECIPE FOR SATAY SAUCE

Cooking traditional satay sauce is a laborious and time-consuming process. It involves pounding spices and peanuts into a fine paste using a pestle and mortar. Here is a quick recipe for time-pressed satay fans.

Ingredients

1 can coconut milk

½ cup crunchy peanut butter

½ small onion, grated

1 tablespoon dark soy sauce

2 teaspoons brown sugar

½ teaspoon red pepper flakes

Method

Combine the ingredients in a saucepan. Heat over medium heat, stirring frequently. Bring to a boil. Remove from heat and keep warm before serving with your favourite satay assortment.

WORLD'S MOST POWERFUL PASSPORT (ALMOST)

The best passports (for visa-free travel) to hold in 2020 are:

1. Japan (191 destinations)

2. Singapore (190)

3. South Korea, Germany (189)

4. Italy, Finland, Spain, Luxembourg (188)

5. Denmark, Austria (187)

6. Sweden, France, Portugal, Netherlands, Ireland (186)

7. Switzerland, United States, United Kingdom, Norway, Belgium (185)

8. Greece, New Zealand, Malta, Czech Republic (184)

9. Canada, Australia (183)

10. Hungary (181)

*The above list is accurate as of July 2020.

Source: CNN Travel

INDEX

A

acronyms 89
advertisements 61, 68
Ah Meng, orangutan 69
AIDS 45
air steward, first 48
Architecture 36
Armenians 150
Aviation 29

B

baby boom 103
baby making 134
baggage claim 39
Balestier 84
Banks 44
Batman 138
biodiversity 88, 109
Board of Censors 21
bombing 51
Bookshops 12
Bras Basah Road 134
bridges 86, 87
bronze elephant statue 29
Bukit Brown 58
Bukit Merah 97
bungalows 132
burials 86, 89
bus, longest 120
Buses 19

C

campaigns 11, 50, 108
caning 69
Capitol Theatre 141
Car ownership 16
casino 101
Cathay, The 151
Causeway 77
Cavenagh Bridge 87
Certificate of entitlement (COE) 16
Changi Airport 39, 104
Chao Tzee Cheng, Dr 75

Chew, Paddy 45
Chief Justices of Singapore 51
CHIJMES 140
chilli crab 155
Chinatown 111, 137, 141
Chinese funeral traditions 79
Chinese New Year 46, 70
Chinese storyteller 25
Chinese surnames 47
Church of Our Lady of Lourdes
      147
Church of St Gregory the
      Illuminator 28, 150
City Day 116
climate 136
clubs and societies 76, 88
coffee 35, 76, 111
Cold Storage 143
Covid-19 31
criminals 86
crops of old Singapore 32
Cultural Medallion Awards 140
curry murder 132

D

dental clinic, first 99
diet 61
diseases 45, 63, 85
durians 78, 156

E

economy 95
Education 55
Election 53
Electronic Road Pricing (ERP) 20
employers 120, 154
endangered species 56
Esplanade 79, 101
extinct species 49

F

Faber, Captain Charles Edward 42

Fandi Ahmad 125
farms 91
film ratings 148
films 18, 21, 74
Food courts 42
food fads 98
foods, local 7, 55, 59, 92, 93, 132,
      155, 157
foreign views 110
forensic 75
funeral rituals 121

G

gambling 102
Geography 29
ghost month 5
gift ideas 31
Goods & services tax 74
Government Hill 65
government matchmaker 27
Grand Prix, F1 49
Great Singapore Workout 106

H

Habib Noh bin Mohamad Al-
      Habshi 33
hawker food 64
Hamilton, Alexander 119
Health 31, 43
Health, psychological 43
heartlanders 146
Henderson Waves Bridge 36
Hill Street Police Station 156
Hilton Hotel 143
historical buildings 28, 141, 147,
      156
Hokkien Mee 132
Hong Lim Park 137
Hotels 5
Housing 13
Housing Development Board
      (HDB) 56, 65, 97, 138
hygiene rating 81

I

ice cream   136, 143
Income tax   60
Inequality   23
insults   7
Internet   121
Internet activities   135
Inuka, polar bear   13
Istana   28, 149

J

Japanese cemetery   86
jargon, local   92
jury system   99

K

kampongs   106
Katong   139
karung guni   120
Kings of Singapore   125
Kucinta cat   24

L

landfill   56
Law   71
Lee Hsien Loong, Prime Minister
   6
Lee Kuan Yew   6, 25, 131
lighthouses   77
lightning strikes   145
loitering   139

M

Madras chunam   63
maids   154
Maintenance of Parents Act   141
Malay proverbs   96
Marina Barrage   146
Marina Bay Sands   101, 102, 151
marriages   83, 98, 107
Mass Rapid Transit (MRT)   115,
   144
Merdeka lions   22
Merlions   147

migratory birds   97
Milestones   81
millionaires   16
Minister, woman   20
Miscellaneous Offences Act   107
Misuse of Drugs Act   52
mixed parentage   98
mobile services   50
Monopoly, Singapore style   113
monuments   79
mooncakes   30
Mount Faber   36, 42
music   156
musicals   60
myopia   148

N

National Anthem   9
national flag   90
National Parks Board   14
National Museum of Singapore
   84, 90, 123
National University of Singapore
   113
Ngiam Tong Boon   10

O

Orchard Road   143
orchids   68, 91
Otters   75

P

pandas   129
Papal visit   25
paranormal activity   38, 83, 105
Parkview Square   151
performance arts venues   17
Pesta Sukan   54
pets   67
pillar boxes   80
plastic   43
plastic surgeon   133
population   67, 96, 138
President of Singapore   48
presidential elections 53
Prime Ministers   6

prisoner art   119
prisoners   119
public holidays   149
Public housing   13
Public transport   19
Pulau Hantu   127
Pulau Semakau   56

Q

Qing Ming   12
Quarries   6
Queenstown   88
The Quests   133

R

Raffles, Sir Thomas Stamford
   statue of   47
Raffles Hotel   10, 28, 49, 51, 68
raining fish   142
Ramlee, P.   136
red light districts   7
religions   104
reservoirs   20
rickshaws   15
Riots   37
roads and expressways   75, 103
Robin Hood   33
Roti John   59

S

samsui women   34
Santry, Denis   28, 79
satay sauce   157
school mottos   113
Scouts & scouting   14
secret societies   117
seditious tombstone   26
Sentosa   118
sex change   147
Sim, Jack   24
Singapore   42, 59
   building names   27
   currency   130, 150
   first newspaper in   142
   firsts in   108-109
   national pledge   18
   people of   8

world records   128
Singapore Airlines   29, 87, 134, 152
Singapore Art Museum (SAM)   28
The Singapore Chronicle   142
Singapore Citizenship Ordinance   133
Singapore Federation of Chinese Clan Association   37
Singapore River   103, 135
Singapore Sling   10, 114
Singapore Standard Time   142
Singapore Stone   22
Singapore Zoo   69, 139
Singaporeans   16, 135
    psyche of   57, 82-83
Singlish   35, 40-41, 107
sitcoms   117
SMS   140
snakes   66
Social Development Unit (SDU)   27
Social Development Service (SDS)   27
Speakers' Corner   137
Speakers of Parliament   80
Special education   55
spoken languages   145
Sports   54, 125
St Andrew's Cathedral   28
Stamford Road   127
stamps   19, 91, 145
street art   94
street names   84, 126-127
Sultan Mosque   28, 53
The Swallows   156

T

tallest buildings   13, 127
Tan Howe Liang   95
Tan Kim Seng   79
Tan, Dr William   15
Tanjong Pagar Railway Station   129
tapioca   43, 44
Taxation   60, 74
Television   46
Telok Ayer Street   64, 100
Telok Blangah Hill   36, 42
Thaipusam   112
Theemithi (fire-walking)   144
Thian Hock Keng temple   64, 100
tigers   112
toilets   24
tourist attractions   102, 122-124
tutors   140
traditional Chinese medicine   23
transport   35
trees   14, 57, 62

U

ultra-marathon   137
urban legends   99

V

visas   157
void decks   97

W

Ward, Frank Dorrington   36
wartime cuisine   39
washing machines   151
wastes   56, 58
water   48
waterfalls   54
weather   17
wedding vows with sign language   154
weddings of the dead   83
wet markets   19
Whampoa Ice House   85
women graduates   118
World Toilet Association   24
Wu, Woffles   133

Y

yusheng   46, 70

PHOTO CREDITS

Line drawings by Ah Bock.
p 80   iStockphoto

The publisher would also like to thank Jeffrey Ng for clarifying legal phrasing on page 52-53.